Modern life

'Are we nearly there yet?'

What is ...
an Indigo Child?

OUT IN THE WILDER reaches of New Age philosophy lies the concept of Indigo Children. Opinion is divided as to whether these children are reincarnated Atlanteans, but on the main point there's impressive consensus. The Indigos, as they're known in the trade, represent a new phase in human evolution. Not only that, but with their psychic powers, warrior spirit and penetrating spiritual wisdom, they're all set to lead mankind into a bright new future.

The phenomenon was first spotted by Nancy Ann Tappe in the 1970s. As a 'parapsychologist, synaesthete and psychic', Tappe was no stranger to reading other people's auras. But then she started to notice something surprising: more and more people born since the Sixties had auras that were indigo – a shade previously unknown in the aura business and associated, significantly enough, with clairvoyance. The human race, Tappe decided, was poised for a great leap forwards.

Even so, it wasn't for another couple of decades that the concept caught on more widely – which is where the story takes a turn for the weird. Since 1989, Lee Carroll, originally a sound engineer, had been channelling Kryon, an angelic entity from the Central Sun who belongs to the same family as the Archangel Michael. (Kryon's aim, as you might imagine, is 'to help humans ascend to a higher vibrational level'.) Because of his Kryon work, Carroll was already a New Age star when, in 1999, he and Jan Tober published *The Indigo Children: The New Kids Have Arrived*. The book picked up Tappe's ideas to announce 'perhaps the most exciting, albeit odd, change in basic human nature that has ever been observed and documented.'

Carroll and Tober also had reassuring news for those of us whose aura-reading is below par. 'You can't mistake the look of an Indigo Child's eyes and face,' they pointed out: 'Very old, deep and wise.' You can look out, too, for children possessing such key Indigo characteristics as an innate resistance to authority, a strong sense of entitlement, a wild imagination and a tendency to get bored easily –

Indigos are so psychically sensitive that they're often disruptive at school and misdiagnosed with Attention Deficit Hyperactivity Disorder...

although some cynics have suggested that none of this makes them very different from the non-Indigo type. On a more sombre note, Carroll and Tober explained how Indigos are so psychically sensitive that they're often disruptive at school and misdiagnosed with Attention Deficit Hyperactivity Disorder. (Those same cynics, sad to say, see this as a handy way of allowing gullible parents to see bad behaviour as a sign of their offspring's special gifts.)

Now, twelve years later, if you type 'Indigo Children' into Google you get 385,000 matches – many for forums in which Indigos discuss the problems of having supernatural powers. Nonetheless, what must be really depressing for rationalists is how mainstream all this stuff has become. *The Indigo Children* and its sequels have sold over half a million copies. Believers in the notion have appeared on Oprah and Richard and Judy. Carroll himself is regularly asked to present his ideas (or possibly Kryon's) at the UN's Society for Enlightenment and Transformation.

There have also been worldwide Indigo conferences, and a successful Indigo documentary and feature film, both produced by James Twyman, whose book *Emissary of Light* describes how in the 1990s he bumped into a master and twelve disciples in the mountains of Bosnia. They were, it duly turned out, members of an ancient secret society who'd handpicked him to proclaim that the world was on the verge of a major awakening.

Which just leaves the question of what Indigos actually do to transform the world and its inhabitants. On the whole, even the most bullish experts get a bit coy here, taking refuge in windy generalities about 'rebuilding all aspects of human life'. Fortunately, Nancy Ann Tappe, back these days at the forefront of the movement, is less vague. It's thanks to Indigos, she says, that we now have Facebook and Twitter. (After all, 'platforms for social interacting are entirely Indigo processes.') And with the Williams sisters and Tiger Woods apparently among their ranks, they also seem pretty good at revolutionising sport. Most startling of all, they may have real power at last – because the most prominent Indigo Child of our time is none other than Barack Obama.
JAMES WALTON

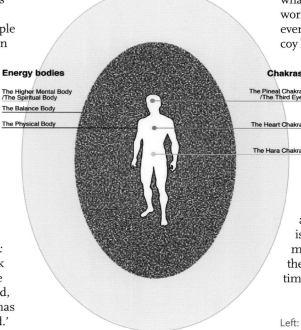

Energy bodies

The Higher Mental Body /The Spiritual Body

The Balance Body

The Physical Body

Chakras

The Pineal Chakra /The Third Eye

The Heart Chakra

The Hara Chakra

Left: the Indigo aura in a nutshell. Any the wiser?

Olden life

What was ...
Mulhall?

EVERY GENERATION has an appetite for freakish facts, for barmy statistics. Today if you want to know how many men are killed annually by their lawnmowers, or how much you could win in bounty payments by shopping the world's top ten criminals, you turn to one of the bestselling compilations by Ben Schott. If our grandfathers wished to know the weight of a 'Scotchman's' brains, or how much carbonic acid was exhaled hourly by a criminal on a treadmill, they found the answer in 'Mulhall', the well-loved *Dictionary of Statistics*, first published in 1884 by Michael George Mulhall. It was then the largest single-volume statistical work in the world. By 1899 it claimed to contain 'all the known statistical data from the time of the Emperor Diocletian down to 1890'. Its Table of Millionaires began with the philosopher Seneca, reputedly worth £3,500,000. You won't find him in Schott's lists of richest men.

Beard alert: Michael George Mulhall

Mulhall, a Dublin-born journalist and number-cruncher reared in South America, is treated with cautious respect in the *Oxford Dictionary of National Biography*, which describes him as 'unique in his time as an individual compiler', in contrast to those who depended on government

> ## Mulhall was not afraid to pass social comment. Why, he wondered, were 19 per cent of the nobility childless?

statistical bureaux. As a Fellow of the Statistical Society he could turn out a History of Prices or a Balance Sheet of the World with the stodgiest of them, but his appeal was that he 'offered data in a manner suitable for popular comprehension'.

He liked nothing better than to compare the heights, weights, aptitudes and short-comings of different classes of society. Eton and Harrow boys were taller than military orphans and boys from industrial schools. Fellows of the Royal Society were, on average, 3.9 inches taller and 21 pounds heavier than 'burglars and other convicts'. How long did it take for people to drink themselves to death? The answers: women 15 years; gentlemen 16; the working classes 18 (the workers lasted longer by sticking to beer). Only one ploughman in a thousand died of intemperance, as against 23 commercial travellers, 38 cab drivers and 55 publicans.

Mulhall was not afraid to pass social comment. He was unhappy about the tendency of his countrymen to marry their aunts and nieces (notoriously, they had also taken to marrying their deceased wives' sisters). Why, he wondered, were 19 per cent of the nobility childless? In Paris 230 spoon-fed infants died for every 100 raised on the breast. French girls were a bit of a puzzle: those with blue eyes reached sexual maturity six months later than those with dark eyes. Of more interest to Mulhall was the work capacity of young women, as determined by their chest measurements. His 'Table of Growth of Telegraph Girls (English)' showed that a girl of 13 could lift 182 pounds, presumably not all at once; in Italy a ten-year-old girl could draw (pull) 80 pounds and an 18-year-old 155 pounds.

Mulhall reached far and wide for his figures. 'The caravans from Berber to Suakim,' he recorded, 'use camels carrying 600 pounds which travel three miles an hour and earn one penny (English) per mile.' The Tsar's 'wood police', numbering 27,000, chopped one and a half tons of firewood daily. Perhaps Mulhall's most eye-popping entry concerns the disgraceful Jukes family. The founder member was an English ne'er-do-well who emigrated to America in 1720. Seven generations later a check on 709 of his descendants showed that 76 were criminals, 128 prostitutes, 142 vagabonds and 131 'blind, insane and otherwise infirm', which appeared to show that a tendency to produce treadmill-fodder was hereditary. *Collier's Encyclopedia* says that over that period the Jukes family cost New York state $1,250,000, but that later investigations showed that its members had improved 'socially and economically'. If your name is Jukes, do not fret – that was not their real name.

E S TURNER

'They keep laughing at us. Bastards'

★ ★ ★ ★ ★ ★ ★ ★ ★ ★ ★ ★ ★ ★ ★ ★ ★

ILLUSTRATION BY HEATH

★ Great Bores of Today ★

'... I've seen every one of them and I've got all the DVDs but out of all of them the best one by far is Goldfinger you remember? he's the one with the white cat or is that Dr No? I always say there was no one as good as Sean whatsisname in those early ones although I liked the one in Never Say Diamonds Again I think that was Roger Moore or was it the other bloke who used to be a male model? that one in New Orleans was good with the car chase and they blow up the helicopter and Bond ends up with the girl in Venice what's her name...?'

© **Fant and Dick**

I once met...

Lord Goodman

EDWARD MIRZOEFF *recalls a time when the big man was lost for words*

'I am the finest after-dinner speaker in the land. There is no need for me to write anything down in advance. And certainly no need for you, young man, to tell me what to do or how to do it.' With jowls quivering, the intimidating bulk that was Lord Goodman swept my protests aside. It was the summer of 1974. The BBC had invited the celebrated solicitor, reputed to be of infinite subtlety, wisdom and behind-the-scenes political influence, to give the annual Richard Dimbleby Lecture. I was the producer.

A year before, Sir Robert Mark, Commissioner of the Metropolitan Police, had given a coruscatingly delivered lecture he called 'Minority Verdict'. Beforehand, with the help of a young barrister called Lennie Hoffmann (now Lord Hoffmann, a former senior Law Lord), he had composed draft after draft. For months he re-wrote, revised and rehearsed. After all, the lecture was fifty minutes long at prime time on BBC1 – and it was live.

Lord Goodman proposed to dispense with all that and go it alone. I told my head of department that Goodman was adamant – a prepared script was not necessary. He warned Brian Cowgill, controller of BBC1 who, in turn, referred up the ladder to the managing director, Huw Wheldon.

From on high the answer came down. If the great man says he is happiest speaking off the cuff, so be it. But I didn't like it.

I went back to Goodman's over-upholstered flat in Portman Place. When he lumbered in I explained that standing in a studio before a cold audience and five large television cameras was not like telling some jolly tales after a good dinner; that fifty minutes was a remarkably long time to fill; that a live broadcast was a tense business, even for television professionals.

Goodman shrugged away my fears. Had he not told me already that no speaker was more experienced or more in demand? There would be no scripts, no rewrites, no rehearsals, no editorial preparation. I had a horrible sinking feeling.

There would be no scripts, no re-writes, no rehearsals, no editorial preparation – I had a horrible sinking feeling

On Tuesday 22 October 1974 Lord Goodman turned up at Television Centre. The most recent of his numerous appointments was as chairman of the Housing Corporation, so he would talk about housing. He began confidently enough with a plea for government to deal with the horrors of squalid homes. He called for a passionate approach to help build more houses, control the price of land, inject a sense of urgency into the planning process. But soon he started running out of things to say. He lurched from the cost of Concorde to the value of gala performances at Covent Garden, but when he began to describe the inadequate size of BBC dressing-rooms, I knew all was lost. 'He's blown it – the bugger's blown it!' I heard 'Ginger' Cowgill's down-to-earth Clitheroe voice shouting behind me.

Somehow Goodman got to the end. The applause was desultory, the party afterwards unusually subdued. In the *Daily Telegraph* Christopher Booker called the performance 'lamentable'. I never saw Lord Goodman again.

'With this ring I thee wed...'

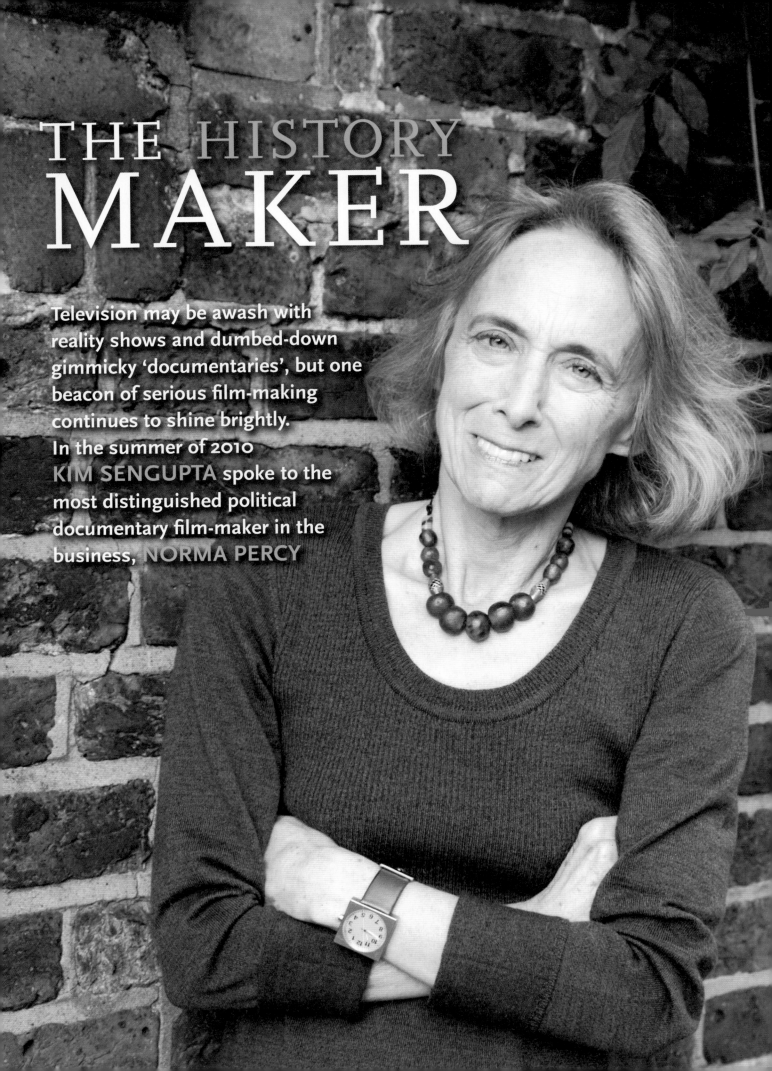

THE HISTORY
MAKER

Television may be awash with reality shows and dumbed-down gimmicky 'documentaries', but one beacon of serious film-making continues to shine brightly.
In the summer of 2010 KIM SENGUPTA spoke to the most distinguished political documentary film-maker in the business, NORMA PERCY

It has been a good twelve months for Norma Percy, winning ten awards in Britain and America and being showered, yet again, with praise. There is also a four-part documentary series in development for the BBC, a likely source of future plaudits.

The new series will be about resurgent Russia, with the working title of 'Putin and the West: The New Cold War'. The BBC normally puts up about half the money – Percy and her team have to raise the rest from American and European sources, not an easy task in the current economic climate. 'To be honest, I don't think there will be the scope for such programmes without the BBC, so obviously we are concerned about what happens to the licence fee,' said Percy, a petite woman of disarming charm, at her office in Kentish Town in north London. 'The way we do these programmes means they take a long time to make and tend to be expensive. But I hope at the end they convey what it was like to be there at some important moments in history.'

If critical acclaim could be translated into funding, Percy need have no worries about the future. BBC Director General Mark Thompson has 'never met anyone as tenacious... she is a benchmark and a role model.' Angus Macqueen, former head of documentaries at Channel 4, describes her work as 'identifying critical moments that the public never see and the politicians never tell you about'. Jack Straw says her programmes are 'extraordinary because of her talent, her imagination, her insight... she is so trusted by everybody, so she gets brilliant access.' The latest gongs Percy has received include the Orwell Prize for lifetime achievement, the Royal Television Society Judges' Award, two Griersons, and several more for her last major project, the series *Iran and the West* (2009).

The Iran series exemplifies the main trademark of her success – revealing the inner tensions and drama behind international realpolitik, obtaining access to the main players and then getting them to describe what took place with remarkable candour. In the series Khatami, Rafsanjani, Jimmy Carter, Madeline Albright, George Shultz, Jack Straw and Vladimir Putin give their versions of Iran's role from the return of Ayatollah Khomeini and the fall of the Shah to the current confrontation over the country's nuclear programme.

The basic history of Iran's fractious relationship with the West, and the US in particular, is well known. What the series does is give a narrative of the decisions which shaped the events. There are also little vignettes, ironic in the light of what was to follow: Ayatollah Khomeini is shown inviting Western journalists to accompany him when he returned in triumph from exile in Paris; a young student leader called Mahmoud Ahmadinejad argues against the taking of American hostages because, for him, the enemy was not the West, but the Soviet Union.

'What we soon discovered was the sense the Iranians felt about being repeatedly let down by America,' says Percy. 'Rafsanjani told us how he had interceded to help the release of American hostages held by the Hezbollah in the Lebanon. Bush senior had said "Goodwill begets goodwill", but failed to lift any sanctions against Iran. Khatami told us how the Iranians had helped the Americans target the Taliban in Afghanistan, yet Bush junior then talked about Iran being part of the "axis of evil".'

Persuading people like these to open up was a long, tortuous

'Have YOU any children?'

process. There was deep anxiety during the making of the Iran programmes that time was rapidly running out. 'There were massive restrictions and genuine fear even among former very senior figures about talking to the foreign media,' Percy recalls. 'One of our biggest funders pulled out because they decided we would not get Rafsanjani. In the end, Khatami probably talked because he knew the Western leaders were talking and he wanted to get his own account in. We told him this was the fairest hearing he was going to get. Rafsanjani probably agreed to be interviewed because Khatami had talked. I guess it was to do with opposing factions in Iranian politics having their say. We have found over the years that asking people to describe what happened, without forcing our own interpretation through commentary or aggressive questions, is the way to get the maximum amount of information.'

Percy began learning her craft from Brian Lapping, then a producer for Granada Television. Born in New York, she had arrived from America to study for an MPhil on British politics at the London School of Economics. Her journey into filmmaking was unplanned: 'I was really interested in politics and got a job in the Commons with the Labour MP John Mackintosh. He was asked by Brian if he knew a researcher who could help him on a programme about Parliament called *The State of the Nation* and he put my name forward. Until then I had no interest at all in working for TV.'

> *She reveals the inner tensions and drama behind international realpolitik, obtaining access to the main players and then getting them to describe what took place with remarkable candour*

What became clear is that public figures who may appear initially reticent are, underneath, actually keen on their imprimatur in history being recorded. The success of the Parliament programme led, in 1982, to the commissioning of a 14-hour series on British decolonisation, *End of Empire*, which brought the team into contact with international leaders: 'A really fascinating, intoxicating experience. I knew which way I wanted to go from then on,' says Percy.

In 1988 Percy followed Lapping when he started his own independent production company, which became Brook Lapping. They made a series of seminal documentaries charting the main global political events of the time, including *Watergate*, *Death of Yugoslavia* and *Endgame in Ireland*.

One series led to another. While filming Bill Clinton for the series on Northern Ireland she saw a photo of him with Ehud Barak and Yasser Arafat taken at the time of the Camp David talks.

Continues ☞

She asked him about it and it became obvious from his answer that he fretted about the fact that he had failed to bring lasting peace to the Middle East. Percy thought, 'This is it, a great story, we have got to tell it, get him to tell it.' Three years later the BBC commissioned *Elusive Peace*.

Listening to the various parties in a conflict led, in many cases, to Percy and her team experiencing a degree of empathy. This did not happen, however, with Slobodan Milosevic, whose interview had been obtained with the help of his formidable wife, Mira. 'He was evasive. We had interviewed Tudjman [the then Croatian leader] who told us about a meeting in which he carved up Bosnia with Milosevic. This was denied, among many other things, by Milosevic. But he knew that we knew. We were to find out later that on the day we filmed his interview, as he protested his innocence, the Srebrenica massacre was taking place.'

'On the day we filmed Milosevic's interview, as he protested his innocence, the Srebrenica massacre was taking place'

The next series on Russia should come out 20 years after Brook Lapping's first big BBC production, *The Second Russian Revolution*, which was about Gorbachev and the fall of the Soviet Union. Putin will be the central character. 'We certainly need to speak to him – this is very much his story. We have spoken to his people and we are hopeful,' Percy muses. 'The BBC has said it wants to schedule it for September 2011. That may seem a long way off, but you really do need all that time to do the kind of thing we do. After that, we are quite keen to look at Iraq and Afghanistan.'

What is the future for expensive documentary producers in the changing broadcasting climate, where cheapness and the lowest common denominator appear to be the ruling factors? 'Obviously funding will be an issue. But I remember the BBC once brought out a series about an aircraft carrier and we were told that was the face of the future, it would all be reality TV, and the type of documentaries we did were finished. That was 30 years ago and we are still here. I think there is still a place for programmes which try to get under the surface of news to understand what makes history. There are lessons to be learned which will affect what happens in the future.'

The joy of sex education
Notes from the sofa

Written and illustrated by **RAYMOND BRIGGS**

VENEREAL DISEASE cast a shadow over my adolescence and no doubt over thousands of other teenagers at the time. Having had not one word of sex education at primary or secondary school, not a single word from parents, my complete ignorance made me vulnerable to every suggestion and rumour.

Throughout the 1940s there were posters everywhere showing the huge letters V and D casting dark shadows across the faces of young servicemen and women. They were quite frightening. To a thirteen-year-old who knew nothing whatever about either the sex or the disease, anything was possible. Had I got it? I used to lie awake at night, focussing my mind on the letters V and D and imagining the words YES or NO floating towards me, hoping for some sort of answer.

Then my friend Pfeff and I came across a small booklet in a newsagent's called *The Red Light*. It told you all about IT, not just about the disease, but IT as well. The booklet cost one and ninepence, so Pfeff and I agreed to form a joint company and to invest tenpence ha'penny each. We then tossed a coin and the loser had the embarrassing ordeal of entering the shop and asking for this shameful volume. Pfeff lost and so emerged from the shop, scarlet in the face, but triumphantly clutching the booklet.

We were in Fleet Street at the time, so we walked up to St Paul's and sat in one of the pews to read the book.

Syphilis you get a discharge (an older boy at school had told me that if you get stuff coming out of it you've got VD), gonorrhoea you get a sore... but then we were suddenly filled with joy: we couldn't have it because we hadn't done IT! You had to do IT to get it. Hooray! We were OK! We thumped one another on the shoulders and bounced up and down on our seats.

An attendant came over and glowered at us as he thought we were larking about. So we crept away like good little boys and walked sedately towards the Whispering Gallery. Until that moment I had had no idea that Pfeff had VD worries as well. We'd probably both been too embarrassed to even mention it to one another.

We climbed a long way up the narrow stone staircase, then an even narrower passage led off to the left, with a rope across it saying NO ENTRY. Naturally, we ducked under the rope and went on and up. This led to a heavy door which we pushed open. When we stepped outside we found ourselves on the roof of the nave, the huge towers in front of us and the massive dome above us. After the dark narrow passage, the space and dazzling light were almost frightening, but with the birds wheeling around in the blue sky, it was exhilarating too. We ran about all over the enormous roof, bigger than our school playground, waving our arms at the birds.

The space! The light! We're on top of St Paul's! And we haven't got VD!

TOP CHUMPS

Yes, *Oldie* readers love Top Chumps!! Simply cut out the Chumps below and glue them to a suitable hard backing. Buy *The Oldie* regularly and you'll be amazed how soon you have a complete set of Top Chumps – ready to do battle with your top CHUMS!!
Get collecting now to make sure of a complete set!!

BORIS JOHNSON

CHUMPFILE
- ★ Tousled hair — 99%
- ★ Faux-buffoon act — 99%
- ★ Extramarital malarkey — 99%
- ★ Silly cycle-helmet — 89%
- ★ Strange father — 99%
- ★ Foot in mouth — 100%

PIERS MORGAN

CHUMPFILE
- ★ Mirror shares scandal — 100%
- ★ Clarkson punch-up — 90%
- ★ Pughe-Morgan surname — 95%
- ★ Doctored Iraq photos — 100%
- ★ Bogus diaries — 94%
- ★ Crap TV programmes — 125%

NAOMI CAMPBELL

CHUMPFILE
- ★ Air hostess assault — 100%
- ★ Maple syrup and pepper diet — 86%
- ★ Chauffeur punching — 99%
- ★ 'Blood diamond' scandal — 95%
- ★ Substance abuse — 96%
- ★ Catwalk collapse — 100%

SARAH, DUCHESS OF YORK

CHUMPFILE
- ★ Toe-sucking scandal — 105%
- ★ Embarrassing father — 86%
- ★ Hideous makeover — 60%
- ★ Paedophile debt payer — 55%
- ★ Accused of plagiarism — 13%
- ★ 'Duchess of Pork' nickname — 60%

JEREMY PAXMAN

CHUMPFILE
- ★ Sneering manner — 93%
- ★ Underpants whinge — 105%
- ★ Love of fish — 96%
- ★ Boring history books — 98.5%
- ★ 7-figure salary — 90%
- ★ Self-importance — 95%

SARAH PALIN

CHUMPFILE
- ★ Children with silly names — 100%
- ★ 'Alaska next to Russia' — 96%
- ★ Hockey mom — 98%
- ★ Fancied by Enfield Senior — 95%
- ★ Maternity 'cover up' — 88%
- ★ Jesus freak — 99%

BLEEPED OUT

It was her big moment – but **ZENGA LONGMORE** *could only watch helplessly as her star acting opportunity went down the Tube*

Illustrated by Martin Honeysett

Those of you who are suffering from over-stressful jobs will glean comfort from reading about my recent work experience. The job was an acting one, advertising a local paper, which I shall refer to as the *Daily Bleep*. At last! Fame, money, invitations to the Jerry Springer show. Anyway, as it turned out, the advert was not to be filmed, but to be performed on a Tube train. The advertising company preened itself on having devised so innovative a coup. Has any other product been advertised live on the Tube before?

I was paired up with a fellow thespian by the name of William, who was

required to don a bowler hat and a pin-striped suit, and carry a quality newspaper under his arm. Our script went somewhat as follows:

William (*standing at the end of the carriage*): Sorry to break the unwritten law of silence on the British Tube, but I just have to say that I have bought my newspaper in good faith, but it is not giving me the interesting news I want!

Me (*from the other end of the carriage, waving my newspaper*): I have all the news I want in *my* paper, because I read the *Daily Bleep*!

The script then became rather technical, describing the latest political shenanigans, business news and travel

updates overflowing in the *Daily Bleep*, but lacking in William's newspaper. The whole scene was to last but one stop. We were asked to work for seven hours, thus performing hundreds of scenes with which to thoroughly hammer the virtues of the *Daily Bleep* into the receptive heads of thousands of commuters. The rates of pay soared to the heights only advertising companies can scale, and we were assured of a full house and a captive audience. It was satisfying to know that, for the first time in my acting career, I would be able to complete a speech without anyone walking out in the middle. And if the train stopped in a tunnel, all the better; my performance would have a chance to be brilliantly embellished. The possibilities for stretching my acting skills were limited only by my imagination, and the length of each stop.

As William and I stepped onto the Tube for our first performance, I experienced that heady rush of adrenalin so familiar to all great divas. Sarah Bernhardt, I have been told, sensed a similar feeling each night before every performance of *Hamlet*.

The train rattled out of the station, and I sat, with quivering fingers gripping my *Daily Bleep* in delicious anticipation. William stood stock still, bowler-hatted and grim. Our audience consisted of three teenage punks with nuts and bolts through every spare inch of visible flesh, five American tourists, who instantly whipped out cameras and camcorders to point at William ('Holy Shamoley! A gen-u-ine Briddish guy in a bowler!'), and a dishevelled Eastern European man with a long-suffering expression. Not what you might call a full house, but for all I knew one of the Americans was an in-law of some great Hollywood mogul. Perhaps I was about to be discovered. I closed my eyes and waited for my partner's opening lines.

Two seconds later, a rich voice rose over the clanking din. 'Pleeease! I have wife and three children and no home! You must help! Just a few coins!'

What on earth had happened? This must have been one of the worst fluffs in the history of Tube theatre!

Turning my head I saw that William was gazing speechlessly at the dishevelled man, who stood before the passengers waving his arms with far more charisma than any mere actor could summon. This man had star quality! 'Just give a few pence.' The Americans tucked their cameras out of sight, and the punks stared at him in terror. Well, that put the kibosh on our opening night. Just as well the critics had stayed away.

The beggar got off at the next stop, and the train proceeded to rattle along. I took a deep breath. Now, at last, my big moment had arrived.

We boggled off into the tunnel. Silence, except for a loud 'dig-a-de-dig' sound. I tried to catch William's eye, but he stubbornly refused to meet my gaze. We continued to travel in silence, me with my *Daily Bleep* loyally held aloft, and William with his bowler hat the object of veiled titters from the other passengers. After half an hour I subtly approached him and signalled to him to get off at the next station.

'William! What's wrong? Why aren't you speaking your lines?'

'Speaking my lines? How can I speak my lines with such an audience? Where's the tension? The drive? I can't possibly begin my speech in an artistic vacuum. When I get an audience with a fuller poetic awareness, then I shall begin my performance.'

'All right then, but we've already done one lap round the Circle Line, and we are being paid to advertise the *Daily Bleep* – and with better money than we'd get at the RSC, I might add!'

William gave me a withering look as if to say, 'Have you no soul?' and we climbed onto the next train.

Our audience consisted of three teenage punks, five American tourists and a dishevelled man – not what you might call a full house

The next lap around the Circle Line proved equally unfruitful. William gazed into space, lips pursed. Just as we pulled out of Liverpool Street for the third time, I became unbearably frustrated at having my big moment wrenched from my grasp, and boldly took matters into my own hands. Shouting clearly above the train's clatter, I fed William his lines.

'What newspaper are you reading, my good man? I am sure it could not be nearly as interesting as the *Daily Bleep*! Do you have the latest political moves, transport news and fashion update like the *Daily Bleep* does?'

All eyes of the passengers fell upon me. All, that is, except William's, who stared into the middle distance, then turned his back in a marked manner.

EE BAH GUM
MIND T'GAP

Northern Line

ROBERT THOMPSON

Sizzling with humiliation I picked up my *Daily Bleep* and continued to ride round and round the Circle Line until lunchtime.

'No! I just can't do it, the feel of the audience just isn't right,' lamented William over his tagliatelle and salad. 'When I was at the Half Moon Theatre in the Mile End Road, it was all so, so different. I was able to engage a dramatic essentialness with my public, but this! Impossible! Can't be done!'

'So you've chickened out completely?'

'Oh no! Of course I will perform, and when I do I shall give of my all, but only when the feel of the audience is right.'

After lunch, we boarded the next Farringdon-bound train with freshly fired verve and energy. Just as we approached the Barbican, the train pulled to an inexplicable halt. William and I exchanged significant glances. The 'feel' of the audience was undoubtedly right. The carriage was filled with learned commuters frowning into airport novels. William cleared his throat, and miraculously his resonant tones filled the carriage, a voice to make the eyes of Laurence Olivier's drama coach moist with admiration.

'I have bought a newspaper, my good people!' he began. All eyes turned upon him. Enquiring eyes. Who is this charismatic man in the bowler hat, the eyes asked, and what does he have to tell us?

'Within this newspaper, what do I find? Do I find informative news? Methinks not! I find –'

'MIND THE GAP!'

His big speech so cruelly interrupted, William threw his arms in the air, showering his audience with pages of that day's quality newspaper, and staggered blindly through the door of the train. His public carried on gaping at this lone figure on the platform until our train chugged eastwards. I bade him goodbye through the window with a feeble wave of my *Daily Bleep*.

The next day, we were supposed to collect our pay cheques. I did not turn up. After all, even actresses have a conscience, and mine would not allow me to accept money for merely sitting all day long on a Tube train, reading the *Daily Bleep*.

As for William, I am not sure whether he felt his non-performance was worth payment. When next I saw him, a few weeks later, he was on the other side of the footlights treading the boards in an Islington pub theatre. When I went backstage to congratulate him on a 'dramatically essential' performance, he pretended to have forgotten who I was.

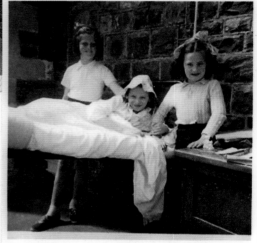

Left: Craig-y-Nos castle, with the open-air balconies (now removed)
Below: Caroline Boyce (foreground), Ann Shaw (in bed) and Mary Davies. Note the tilted bed, a treatment known as 'being on blocks'. Ann was a patient at Craig-y-Nos for four and a half years

The sanatorium children

CAROLINE BOYCE *recalls the twenty months she spent as a child in the austere and isolated Victorian Craig-y-Nos tuberculosis sanatorium in Wales*

It is 1951, and I am ten years old. I am standing with several other small girls at the fourth-floor window of a Welsh Victorian castle, a TB isolation sanatorium. We are waving and calling frantically to our parents, who are waiting far below in the courtyard. At two o'clock precisely they will be allowed into the building, and will clatter upstairs to our ward. The minutes between their entry into the building and their arrival at our bare, curtainless room seem almost as long as the four weeks since we have last seen them.

The building, called Craig-y-Nos (Rock of the Night), is situated many miles from anywhere, on the edge of what is now the Brecon Beacons National Park, and many visitors travelled for hours in buses, taxis and cars, and even walked long distances, to see their children for four hours a month; some children were never visited, and a few were abandoned.

I was admitted to the hospital, formerly the home of the singer Adelina Patti, in November 1949, and was plunged into the austere sanatorium treatment regime of enforced rest, eating and fresh air. Children with skeletal TB were held

rigid for many months in plaster beds of frightening proportions, while others had surgery to immobilise infected lungs. Some lived and slept on balconies in all weathers. My stay lasted twenty months, a comparatively short time; many remained there for several years. Whole families were sometimes admitted and put into different wards. Men and women, boys and girls were strictly segregated. Deaths were not uncommon. TB, one of the most feared diseases of the time, was no respecter of age or station, and carried an enormous social stigma. My com-

as best we could. We drew, wrote letters, stories and diaries, sang songs, invented games and read any book we could get. Occasionally there was a film or a concert in Patti's exquisite little theatre in the castle, and a Christmas pantomime was put on each year by local residents. Education was negligible – two blue-overalled teachers appeared sporadically with sheets of simple sums and a selection of books. The little work we did was collected without comment and never returned. The quality and attitudes of the nursing and medical staff varied.

Children with skeletal TB were held rigid for many months in plaster beds of frightening proportions. TB was one of the most feared diseases of the time

panions in the top ward were from all backgrounds, including a travellers' child, Sybil, whose admittance I remember well. She sobbed miserably and her distraught parents, smelling strongly of wood smoke, had to be driven from the ward.

Our endlessly tedious days were spent resting and trying to amuse ourselves

Some were kind but remote, having been instructed not to form emotional links with the children. Others bordered on the cruel, and treated us in a less than friendly fashion. Apparently some restless younger children were sometimes tied to their beds. One squat, glowering female doctor with a heavy limp petrified us all. A young nurse once put a dead spider in my bed to frighten me, and taunted us with stories of Adelina Patti's ghost wandering the wards at night.

Isolated from families, the companionship of the other children was vital, and strong friendships were forged. As our health improved, we progressed slowly towards being allowed up, wearing our day clothes, for a whole day, and in good weather we walked in the enormous hospital grounds. It gave one a wonderful sense of freedom to be out in the clear air, away from the dreary wards with their stark iron hospital beds. We played among the rhododendron bushes, ran along the wooded paths, and rode the stone deer statues on the terrace.

Going home was strange. Although I was glad to get out of the hospital, it felt odd to be back amongst people I had barely seen for many months. Some ex-patients have said that they felt alone and vulnerable with families they hardly knew, and they sometimes faced hostility from siblings. Others arrived home to find new babies had supplanted them in their absence. I was lonely and felt a certain detachment from my family, who seemed to find me difficult and perplexing. School posed problems too – the formality was hard to cope with after such a long period of sparse education.

The stories of many children at Craig-y-Nos, which ceased to be a hospital in 1960 and is now a hotel, have recently been collected by another ex-patient, Ann Shaw. Her book makes harrowing reading – but it is also funny and uplifting, a testimony to the resilience of the young human spirit when faced with long separation from family and home.

• *The Children of Craig-y-Nos: Life in a Welsh Tuberculosis Sanatorium, 1922–1959* by Ann Shaw and Carole Reeves, £9.99 PB, Wellcome Trust

AIRPORT CAFE

'Sir, you left your Chelsea bun unattended, and it had to be destroyed'

MIND THE AGE GAP

Lizzie Enfield

THE POLISH waitress looks as if she is about to lose her cool. She's been tolerant of my father's attempts to flirt with her.

'Jadwiga.' He reads the badge with her name on. 'An unusual name. Where are you from?'

'Poland,' she says, plonking menus in front of us and disappearing so he can't ask any more.

'What does Jadwiga mean?' He takes up where he left off, when she has taken our order and is gathering the menus.

'Battle,' she says, straightening the cutlery, or drawing battle lines with steak knives – we couldn't be sure which.

My father is silenced and an uneasy truce breaks out. But when we have finished eating, my mother pipes up: 'Can we have a doggy bag?'

'A what?' Jadwiga's tone is defensive.

'A doggy bag,' my mother says again.

'I see my manager,' Jadwiga says and marches towards the kitchen.

'I don't think doggy bag was on the English vocabulary list at night school in Gdansk,' I say.

'Everyone knows what a doggy bag is,' my mother says. But they don't. Until they heard their grandmother ask for one, my children had never come across the term for any container used to take home leftovers for euphemistic dogs.

To them, it seems an odd thing to do. They are totally at ease with waste. Oldies are generally less tolerant. They understand that a food shortage does not simply mean that the man from Waitrose has not yet delivered the weekly shop. Throwing food away is as abhorrent to them as the idea of actually having to eat a whole meal is to my son.

'Don't do that!' my mother will shout at my husband, as he makes himself a cup of tea in her kitchen. He will freeze, teaspoon poised mid-air, balancing a teabag on it, unsure what it is he is not supposed to be doing.

I know. He was about to put the teabag in the bin. But the bin is not for teabags – or much else for that matter. I don't really know why they have one. They certainly tried to resist the local council, when they insisted on depositing

a wheelie bin on their doorstep. 'It's enormous,' my mother protested. 'We don't need it.' They don't. The rubbish they produce would fit in a milk carton.

The teabag my husband thought might go in the bin goes in the compost, the seeds from the melon he's just eaten go in the container with scraps for the chickens, the dish I am about to wash up must not be washed because the dog (a real one) has not yet been given the chance to lick the remains, and the congealed fat in the bottom of the roasting dish will probably be used to make soap.

So it is hardly surprising that my mother wants something in which she can take home our leftovers. 'Does she have to ask?' My daughter is at the anxious age where anything remotely embarrassing, especially if the perpetrator of the embarrassment is a relative, brings her out in a rash.

When Jadwiga comes back she has the bill and a look on her face which dares anyone to stop her clearing our plates away.

'You wouldn't think we were in the middle of a credit crunch,' my mother remarks as we leave, as if the very fact of it should have brought on a doggy bag renaissance. 'I don't know what to give the dog for her supper now.' I am sure the no-waste waste system will yield up some appetising leftovers.

On my walk home I bump into a friend who is propping up his bicycle outside a newsagent. Strapped to the carrier is a small box.

'Ooh!' I say, thinking that my mother would be interested to see this little container. It has an opening like a tissue box and is labelled 'Doggy Bags'.

'Do they actually make bags specifically to be doggy bags?' I say to the friend.

'Yes,' he says. 'More and more councils are fining people who don't clear up after their dogs. These bags are biodegradable, so they're better than plastic ones.'

'Oh,' I say again, as it dawns on me why the waitress may have thought a doggy bag was a strange request...

Lost in Venice

Before his death in 2006, travel writer **ERIC NEWBY** *visited the stinking beautiful city*
Pictures by John Ward, RA (1917–2007)

Whenever I come back to this utterly enslaving, beautiful, sinking, sometimes stinking, city, I do so with the hope that this time it will yield up its secrets to me. But when the time comes for me to leave I realise that even if I stayed in it for the rest of my life this could never be. If Venice is a labyrinth, it is one in which you can wander for ever without any hope of reaching the centre, for the simple reason that, as a labyrinth, it has no centre and, as in a labyrinth, you will be lucky to escape from it without a pair of fallen arches. But really Venice is not sufficiently substantial to be compared with a labyrinth. It is much more like the mirage which so often confronts the passenger as the ship sweeps in towards the city up the dredged channel from the Adriatic, its domes and campaniles looming up larger than life in the air, then liquefying, dissolving and sometimes dispersing completely before taking on some semblance of substance.

In *Albertine Disparue*, Proust writes of entering a network of *calli*, the little alleyways of the city, and coming by chance upon a great open *campo* in the moonlight and failing to find it again the next day, wondering whether it was part of a dream, or a place like one of those oriental palaces 'to which mysterious agents convey by night a person who, taken home again before daybreak, can never again find his way back to the magic dwelling which he ends by supposing that he visited only in a dream.'

This feeling of a lack of substance, which even the largest Venetian buildings possess, perhaps because they literally rise from the water, is heightened by the apparent emptiness of so many of them. An emptiness you can only experience at night.

Great *palazzi*, some of which are big enough to house a hundred persons, have water gates which look as if they have not been opened for a hundred years. The steps leading up to them are covered with long green weed. Inside, the vast hall is lit, if at all, by a forty-watt bulb. Sometimes there is another, equally feeble light in another room high up under the highest cornice, belonging to the caretaker, or perhaps a hermit. The feeling of emptiness extends far beyond the Grand Canal. It is especially strong in those parts of the city which tourists rarely visit, up in the Quartiere Grimani, in the territory around the Arsenale, in the alleys of San Toma where the cats of Venice reign supreme and there is scarcely a dog to be seen. At night, especially in winter, when they have made their ritual, obligatory *passeggiata* in the principal *calli*, *piazze*, *campi* and *salizade* of whatever neighbourhood they inhabit, the ordinary Venetians disappear completely, leaving the city to visitors and those who live off them. They do this because most of them have to get up hideously early in order to get to work on the terra firma at Mestre or Marghera. So the best way of seeing some is by chugging down the lesser waterways, where you will have fleeting glimpses of them through windows that are almost always barred: of a custodian asleep at a desk in some important archive, a man and a girl kissing, a family sitting round a table to which a risotto is coming in a cloud of steam – like a series of not very modern pictures hung in the open air on walls of leprous stone.

What can you do in Venice? By day, armed with Antonio Salvadori's book, *101 Buildings to See in Venice*, you can discover a lot that you would probably otherwise pass by, including that remarkable enclave of Venetian skyscrapers in the Ghetto.

In Venice, according to the French authors of *Guide Jul-*

If Venice is a labyrinth, it is one in which you can wander for ever without any hope of reaching the centre

liard de L'Europe, there are four intelligent ways to spend the evening. The first, and most costly, is to hire a gondola (a closed model if one has improper thoughts and the means to gratify them); the second is to install oneself at a table in the Piazza San Marco; the third to look for adventure in the streets and alleys; the fourth to go to bed with a good book and a bottle of Scotch. When one has tried all these, the authors say, there are the night clubs.

Venice is a city, night clubs or not, in which it is useful to have enough money. Being penniless in Venice conjures up visions of Baron Corvo, past even pederasty, sleeping on mud banks in the Lagoon and being gnawed by crabs and rodents. Having too much brings Hemingway to mind, with his awful *Across the River and into the Trees*, and his awful Colonel Cantwell.

When should one go to Venice? May is lovely, June is good, July and August insufferable – the greatest crowds, the smelliest smells; the first half of September is culture time, with music and cinema at the Lido; October is good. Winter is strange and exciting, but really wintry winter can be a bit much and the fogs are something Jack the Ripper would have got lost in. A lot of hotels and restaurants close from the end of October to April. The *vaporetti*, the passenger boats that take you around Venice, have become very expensive. How long should one stay in Venice? Never long, but return often to make sure that it has not sunk beneath the waves.

GRANNY ANNEXE

Virginia Ironside

A near-fatal encounter with Cyclops and other Dark Creatures

'Oh, God, it's a nightmare!' I've used that expression so often that it has almost lost its meaning. (Except, of course, when I have real nightmares, which are, I have to say, of the Stephen King variety, with monsters, horrors and, oddly, excellent plots.)

But recently I experienced what really did feel like a nightmare. I had a car crash. Now, I've never had a proper car crash before. I've bumped into people's bumpers and people have bumped into mine, and once a bus scraped my side and once a bunch of manic drug-addicts in a stolen van drove into my parked car and wrote it off, but nothing has ever happened that made me doubt my abilities as a driver.

But last week was different. I was driving home along a semi-motorway at midnight when a man appeared ahead with a flashing red light on his head like a Cyclops. I drove round him and turned my head to look to see what he was warning me about. A body? A fire? A three-headed monster? But my curiosity was my undoing. A moment later I'd crashed full on into the broken-down car he'd been trying to warn me about. My car was a write-off.

It's not a place that most of us are familiar with – the side of an enormous road in the pitch dark, in the freezing cold, and with cars roaring by, lighting you up like a ghost in the headlights before leaving you abandoned. Particularly

When the police arrived, I thought I'd escaped but in my discombobulated state they, too, appeared like alien beings

in the company of a Cyclops whose car you've just driven into. True to the nightmare theme, this man – if, indeed, it was a man – was not remotely perturbed that I'd driven into his car. He just continued signalling wildly to the approaching lights. Even though by now, of course, the danger was far worse, because as well as his broken-down car there was mine as well, sticking out into the middle of the road. If you could still call it a car. It looked more like a crushed and abandoned space vehicle.

While we waited for the police, an enormous lorry thundered by, screeched to a halt, and out of his high cab hopped a kind of Hobbit. He was wearing a woolly hat, he was half-shaven, and his arms, I swear, reached to the ground. Saying nothing, he signalled to Cyclops and between them they moved my car to the side of the road. Then the Hobbit hopped back into his cab and roared off.

When the police arrived I thought

that I'd escaped from my bad dream but in my discombobulated state they, too, appeared like alien beings. You could hardly look at them for blue flashing lights, yellow stripes and curious peaked caps, and when one of them was called from his radio I thought it was him speaking and tried to reply.

We waited an hour for a pick-up truck, an hour I spent in a shocked state, half crying, half gasping, half contemplating 'What if?' – all the while numbly assembling a curious assortment of debris from my car into a string bag to take home with me. Maps. Old tapes. Residents' parking permit. Notices reading 'I have put money into this meter but it doesn't work'. The sat-nav. Curiously, a rape alarm. And, finally, an angel with moving wings, still intact on the dashboard.

Presently, a pick-up lorry arrived with a ramp and the Hobbit's brother (apparently), an oil-smeared, bearded, mumbling Dark Creature, shoved my car onto his lorry and drove off.

At home, over an enormous vodka, I thanked my lucky stars I'd only had a small glass of wine before my journey. That night, and for nights afterwards, I dreamed of crashes. I woke in a sweat. I went by public transport – a revelation. And I ordered a new car.

Now I've put my plastic angel back on the dashboard. I drive like a snail. And I hope never to meet those Night Creatures again. It was, truly, a nightmare.

Notting Hill

What goes up comes down, says **ANDREW HOSKEN**

One of my enduring memories of living in Notting Hill is standing in my kitchen one morning in 1995 watching two prostitutes trying to stab my lodger to death. Luckily for him, he was large with long arms whereas the prostitutes were small and rather unhealthy. He had lured one of them back to my flat and then refused to pay her the measly £25 she had demanded. He was an awful scumbag and I quite enjoyed watching the police throw him and his belongings onto the street. We then tracked down the poor woman and gave her £100 – partly to apologise but also out of deep gratitude for giving me the excuse I needed to reclaim the spare room.

The incident highlighted a short-coming in security which I recti-fied by a call to Phil's Grille and Bill Security Emporium (motto: 'We aim to incarcerate you'). In our part of Notting Hill at that time, most of the law-abiding citizens seemed to live behind bars while all the muggers, burglars and assorted criminals ruled the streets: you had to watch your step. Notting Hill Gate itself had always been rather swanky, but where we lived in North Kensington – sandwiched between Portobello Road and Ladbroke Grove – was edgy: the Notting Hill of Keith Talent and *London Fields* and, not all that long ago, Peter Rachman.

But goodness! Hasn't the old place gone down hill in the ten years since I left? Most nights, my local on Ladbroke Grove was a smoke-filled commotion with drunken old Irish guys scrap-ping in the corner while a barmaid swept up bits of teeth with a dustpan and brush. Now, snooty hedge-funders boast about bonuses over decent claret or a jar of strawberry Belgian beer. The juke box has gone, along with the overpowering smell of Dettol, and the air is filled with the tap-tapping of laptops.

The place teems with brokers and barristers slurping buckets of coffee mocha, the sound of their braying disturbing the peace for miles around

The old couple next door ran an illegal drinking den; the rattling of dominoes drove me to despair most Saturday nights. They've upped sticks back to Jamaica where they live like kings thanks to the fortune they secured for their dingy basement. Down the Portobello Road the heart would sing at the sight of a Salvation Army captain rattling his tin on a cold wet evening outside the derelict old Electric Cinema. Now someone's done the place up and it teems with brokers and barristers slurping buckets of coffee mocha, the sound of their braying disturbing the peace for miles around.

In a recent series, Harry Enfield runs a store called Modern Wank that sells loads of over-priced garbage to gullible people with too much money. There's another antiques store called Old Shit flogging pricey antiques. And that about sums up the current retail sector for Notting Hill.

The demise began in about 1998, when the council introduced resi-dents' parking. Few people understand the social-cleansing power of residents' parking: it is a pure avenging fire which dodgy neighbourhoods can't withstand. To get a permit, you needed proof that you paid council tax, car insurance and road tax. Within months, the tarts, pimps, drug dealers, vagabonds and cut-throats seemed to melt away and in their place came the bankers, the trustafarian fops, the dot-com arseholes, the future Tory front-benchers and the greaseball libel lawyers.

What really finished off the place was the eponymous Richard Curtis movie. It completed the transformation from neighbour-hood to tame tourist safari park. Even the carnival now seems to throb less menacingly and attract more sponsorship.

A few places hold out. You can still find the odd watering hole with people who seem fairly normal. It probably won't last: here, I'm afraid, it's down Notting Hill all the way.

OLIVIA DURDIN-ROBERTSON

The High Priestess of the Temple of Isis is alive and kicking, reports ANTHONY GARDNER

Whatever you might expect to find in an Anglo-Irish dungeon, a Temple of Isis is not high on the list. But follow the kitchen passage at Huntington Castle, push through a pair of painted doors and descend a flight of steps, and you enter a realm where normality seems a faint memory. Here between the brick pillars, where the freezing damp clutches at your sinews, every square foot is given over to curious devotional objects: Egyptian wall hangings; feathered masks; wooden carvings of the female form; spiky crystals; painted ankhs. The main altar is presided over by a gilded goddess balancing a pitcher on her head; lesser ones are banked with candles, fruit and artificial flowers. A Tibetan prayer bell, a harp and a ghetto blaster stand ready to play their ceremonial roles.

The temple is the creation of Olivia Durdin-Robertson and her late brother Derry. Founded on the vernal equinox of 1976, their Fellowship of Isis now claims over 27,000 members around the world. The Fellowship believes in the immortality of the soul and, according to its manifesto, worships the goddess Isis as 'the Divine Mother of all beings – humans, plants, animals, each element and atom, are individualised images of God.' This interconnectivity can be enhanced by meditation and developing the individual's psychic powers, including telepathy. At 92, Miss Durdin-Robertson continues to lead the 'FoI', making annual journeys in her capacity as High Priestess to the USA (to meet the faithful) and England (to visit crop circles).

'I've even been to Japan and seen our ceremonies performed in a Buddhist temple,' she says. 'We have some very, very distinguished members – writers,

Olivia Durdin-Robertson communing with the goddess

painters, people of ideas. Jorge Luis Borges was one of them. We appeal to people not just through spirituality, but through the arts and beauty.'

The Fellowship of Isis believes in the immortality of the soul and worships the goddess Isis as the 'Divine Mother'

She was born in London on Friday 13th April 1917, 'during a Zeppelin raid, with shrapnel raining on the roofs'. On her mother's side she is related to the Graves family ('I was told my cousin Robert was a dreadful man because he wore sandals and lived in sin on a barge with a woman called Laura'), the Honourable Violet Gibson – the subject of a recently published book about

her attempt to shoot Mussolini – and the Earls of Rosse. Her father's family seemed less interesting until *The Da Vinci Code* drew attention to an obscure genealogical work called *Stemmata Robertson et Durdin*: 'They found we were all Merovingians, related to Mary Magdalen, who grew their hair long, conversed with beasts and healed by the laying on of hands.'

With the Troubles raging in Ireland, Olivia was eight before her parents took her to live at the family's ancestral home in County Carlow. According to her spiritual autobiography, *The Call of Isis*, Huntington Castle – a fortified house built in 1625 beside the village of Clonegal – provided her with 'psychic doorways' into another world. On one occasion the gloomy tapestry-covered corridor outside the dining-room led her into a place of brilliant sunshine where she talked to an elderly man with a thin white beard and blue gown sitting beside a mosaic-paved fountain. Her father gave a sympathetic ear to such experiences: 'He was a Freemason and understood about mysticism.'

For many years she pursued a conventional life, studying at art school and enrolling as a nurse during the war, before becoming a social worker in Dublin. Her involvement with deprived children inspired *St Malachy's Court*, the first of half a dozen well-received novels which she published between 1946 and 1956. Her writing skills, however, have long been diverted to the service of the Fellowship, for which she has devised more than a hundred ceremonies, including a version of the Eleusinian Mysteries.

Her brother Derry, who claimed the barony of Strathloch, was ordained in the Church of Ireland, but embraced Isis after a vision in which God appeared to him as a woman; he then devoted himself to compiling an encyclopaedia of goddesses, and removing references to God as a male from all the books in the castle's library.

Huntington, Miss Durdin-Robertson explains, is blessed with strong energies which make it the ideal base for their Fellowship. 'There are some places on earth that are magnetic centres. Here it's because of the meeting of two rivers – the Slaney, the river of healing, and the Derry, the river of grove oaks. That's why we can't ever get rid of people: one man came to stay with my grandfather and didn't leave for thirty years.'

'Rex doesn't seem to like the stew, Mavis'

The Fellowship describes itself as 'multi-religious, multi-racial and multi-cultural'. Its devotees include not just spiritualists, druids and witches, but members of the mainstream religions; its doctrine generously embraces every

goddess and even gods. 'We're all born of the divine, God the mother,' says Miss Durdin-Robertson. 'You respect everything you meet, a caterpillar or whatever, which is what Albert Schweitzer taught – as did St Francis of

Assisi, whom I like very much. What is good is real; the rest is shadows. You have to fight against evil here, but in the next world it doesn't exist.'

Her only interest now, she says, is in 'spiritual ideas and rebirth. What you

Huntington Castle provided Miss Durdin-Robertson with 'psychic doorways' into another world. On one occasion the gloomy tapestry-covered corridor led her into a place of brilliant sunshine where she talked to an elderly man

have to realise is that my family – my mother, father, sister, brother, nephew – are all over there. That's what really matters, you know: linking people – because that's for ever. The other things are all caught up in time.'

JUNE AND GERALD by NAF

Instead of 'Blue rinse perfection', the online book company mistakenly sent this. I'll send it back.

Maybe we could keep it?

I suppose so. I've never tried Indian cooking before.

The tragedy of OTHELLO

Oldie theatre critic **PAUL BAILEY** *remembers Zeffirelli's abysmal 1961 Stratford production*

I spent most of 1961 at the Shakespeare Memorial Theatre in Stratford-upon-Avon as a very lowly member of the company. I was a spear carrier, an attendant lord, and a soldier of sorts. My only identifiable roles were Dennis in *As You Like It* and Lovel in *Richard III*. I was also a silent monk at the beck and call of Max Adrian's Friar Laurence in *Romeo and Juliet* and a mumbling nobody welcoming John Gielgud's Othello to Cyprus.

Othello was the final and most eagerly anticipated play in what had proved to be a disastrous season. The director was Franco Zeffirelli, and Peggy Ashcroft was cast as Emilia. The entire company was excited at the prospect of John Gielgud making theatrical history in the one major role he had never attempted, and the first rehearsals reflected that sense of excitement. Gielgud was not in the least starry. You could tell that this was a challenge he was facing with the utmost seriousness. When he spoke of the 'Anthropophagi, and men whose heads / Do grow beneath their shoulders' it sounded thrilling to us. 'Rude am I in my speech' was a sentiment he expressed with the delicious irony of one whose speech had rarely, if ever, been rude.

What puzzled us onlookers was that Zeffirelli seemed more interested in the actors playing Roderigo, Cassio and Lodovico, whom he was teaching to be overtly Italian in their demeanour. Consequently, there was a surfeit of what is best described as Mediterranean gesturing. Gielgud was too polite to inquire why the director was ignoring him. Perhaps Zeffirelli assumed that such a celebrated actor needed no assistance from him. If that was the case, he was very wrong. Gielgud was always in need of directors, especially those he

respected, such as Peter Brook. As the weeks went by, Gielgud was finding it harder and harder to give vent to his exasperation. Then, one memorable morning, Peggy Ashcroft questioned Zeffirelli's command of English. She was right to do so, but it seemed like heresy at the time. 'Peggy's behaving like an absolute bugger,' Gielgud was

Gielgud and Bannen were hopelessly mismatched, a fact that everybody acknowledged except the vain director

heard to say, but he must have known that she had seen through Zeffirelli's pretentiousness. Things got worse, while Gielgud did the *Times* crossword by putting in answers to the clues of his own invention. He was desperately trying to stay calm. Ian Bannen, an extremely likeable man who addressed anyone he talked to as 'heart', found Iago difficult to memorise and stumbled over his words, to Gielgud's intense frustration. 'Oh God, I can't bloody act with you,' the great man cried out in that wonderful flute-like voice, and the startled Bannen was reduced to mumbling, 'But heart, I'm trying my best, heart.' A minute later, Gielgud apologised for his rudeness, but it was clear that there was to be no rapport between the Moor of Venice and his devious Ancient. Gielgud was at his finest in an ensemble of like-minded and dedicated performers and

Bannen was not of their number: he was an accidental stage actor, by which I mean that he stumbled on his effects instead of planning them and rehearsing them until they attained perfection. Gielgud and Bannen were hopelessly mismatched, a fact that everybody acknowledged except the vain director.

The sets and costumes were 'designed' by someone called Peter J Hall. The clothes were put together from those worn in paintings by Titian, Tintoretto and other Venetian masters. Zeffirelli would point at a reproduction and say 'This one' or 'That one'. There were no designs to speak of, and the cumbersome backdrops were similarly filched from famous paintings. On the first night the audience sat in semi-darkness for twenty minutes while the stagehands changed the scenery from Venice to Cyprus, with unShakespearean shouts

John Gielgud (right) as Othello and Ian Bannen as Iago in the 1961 RSC production at Stratford-upon-Avon

of 'Alf' and 'Fred' as columns were taken down and replaced by more columns. Gielgud, whose face was lightly tanned, Arab-style, was asked to wear brown and black in two scenes in subdued lighting. The effect was to make his features disappear. At the dress rehearsal, I sat in the stalls with Leslie Hurry, one of the finest designers of his day, who remarked that this production was taking the theatre back to the age of Herbert Beerbohm Tree, the actor-manager who put live rabbits on stage in *A Midsummer Night's Dream*.

There were no rabbits at the first performance that November, but there were some grotesquely funny mishaps. Apart from the twenty-minute wait between scenes, there was the moment when Iago said to Othello 'Cassio's dead', to Gielgud's visible consternation. 'No, he's not,' Bannen instantly explained. But this was as nothing to what happened when Gielgud bent down to kiss the dead Desdemona. 'I kiss'd thee ere I kill'd thee, no way but this / Killing myself, to die upon a kiss,' he said, leaving his moustache and goatee beard on Dorothy Tutin's face. Gielgud must have known then that he was starring in the biggest fiasco of his long and distinguished career.

The reviews were viciously cruel. On the fifth night of the short run, Gielgud, standing in the wings, turned to Dorothy Tutin and remarked 'Only thirteen more of the fuckers to go.' He spoke the heartfelt words with a smile, as was typical of his nature. Not long after, Laurence Olivier, who delighted in his old rival's failure, played Othello to immense success. But watch him on film now, and you will see an eyeball-rolling ham who abandons his West Indian way of speaking as soon as the big speeches come. Gielgud was not in the rivalry business and praised Olivier for triumphing where he had failed.

Gielgud's misplaced faith in the 'genius' of Franco Zeffirelli is probably the most important factor in the disaster, along with the genial Ian Bannen's inability to be convincingly evil. But Gielgud was not the man to hide behind excuses. I can only say, fifty-eight years on, that at one rehearsal he moved us all to tears. There was a huge party after the first night – a wake, in reality – attended by Luchino Visconti, Pierre Cardin, Jeanne Moreau and Ingrid Bergman. Gielgud did not show up. But then, he wouldn't have even if he had been cheered to the rafters. He was that kind of modest genius.

NOT MANY DEAD
Important stories you may have missed

As the coach drew away, the Queen pulled a blanket up to guard against the chill and the president of South Africa wiped his nose with a handkerchief.
The Guardian

A planned talk by BBC weather presenter Richard Angwin about the future of weather forecasting has been cancelled due to the weather.
Gazette and Herald (Marlborough and Pewsey edition)

A school has come together to pay its respects to a pet guinea pig which died after a short illness.
Darlington and Stockton Times

Police in Ringwood are investigating the circumstances surrounding an injury to a dog's nose.
Salisbury Journal

A man who was trying to identify an old service station through a photo shown in the *Christchurch Mail* last week has discovered its location.
Christchurch Mail, New Zealand

'The First Wives' Club: Miriam and SamCam wake up to new lives. Mrs Cameron popped into Downing Street while make-up free Mrs Clegg went to work.
Daily Mail website

High levels of alcohol-related crime are now happening in Cromwell. Police are putting it down to excessive alcohol consumption.
Cromwell Bulletin, New Zealand

An oven glove caught fire at a property on Melrose Road, Thringstone.
Loughborough Echo

Jeremy Paxman wears a cycle helmet and signals clearly in central London yesterday.
Daily Telegraph

A police squad has been banned from using toasters due to health and safety concerns.
Liverpool Daily Post

The new Poundland store in the Priory Meadow shopping centre will not open this weekend.
Hastings and St Leonards Observer

The *Antiques Roadshow* team visit Jersey's Samares Manor, where items examined include a lemon squeezer said to have belonged to Marilyn Monroe.
The Independent

Busy Easter predicted on UK roads.
Headline, Telegraph online

Unwrecked England

The Oxford University Museum of Natural History and the Pitt Rivers Museum, Oxford

Candida Lycett Green

These two museums, which lead one to another, comprise one of the most magical places to visit I know. Compact and undaunting, they are an example of just how museums should be. The main building is a rich Ruskinian homage to and celebration of Victorian engineering, art and craftsmanship. Its extraordinarily eclectic mix of artefacts fills you with nothing but wonder, and all the schoolchildren I saw wandering around the museums were alert and interested. You leave the place happier than when you came in.

When Henry Acland, a distinguished local doctor, was made the University Reader in Anatomy, he immediately set about promoting the creation of both a science building and a museum of natural history, with lecture rooms and laboratories attached. In 1849, together with a handful of progressive science professors, he secured the passing of a resolution to build a museum which would gather 'all the materials explanatory of the organic beings placed upon the globe'. One of Acland's oldest and closest friends was John Ruskin, whose strong beliefs in the Gothic and in nature as a source of ornament were upheld from the outset.

Benjamin Woodward, a Dublin architect, was in charge of the overall design and the employment of craftsmen. On the museum's completion in 1860 Ruskin wrote to Acland that it was 'the first building raised in England since the close of the fifteenth century which has fearlessly put to new trial this old faith in the genius of the unassisted workman who gathered out of nature the materials he needed.'

Once inside the double-height courtyard you feel as though you are in some exotic jungle with light pouring through a canopy of trees. The huge expanse of glazed roof is supported by long, thin, clustered columns from which spring elegant spandrels, like branches, each adorned with different wrought leaves, ferns and fronds.

> ## Once inside the double-height courtyard you feel as though you are in some exotic jungle with light pouring through a canopy of trees

The mammoth jawbone of a sperm whale, the spectacular bones of a brontosaur found near Chipping Norton, and the procession of skeletons – elephant, giraffe, horse, bison, deer, rhino and polar bear – marching two by two the length of the courtyard, merge perfectly with the exquisite structural ironwork carried out by Skidmore of Coventry, who were given carte blanche. The capitals of over fifty marble and stone columns around the cloister and the gallery are beautifully carved with naturalistic foliage, fruit and flowers by three Irish masons. They too were given a completely free rein but were eventually sacked for caricaturing various Oxford notabilities in the form of monkeys and cats. The gallery, hung with Japanese paper butterflies, has dioramas of insects and a display of beetles set out like precious jewels in shades of iridescent gold, green, orange and blue.

Acland's achievement in getting the Museum of Natural History built represented the beginnings of modern science at Oxford. Twenty-five years later the father of British archaeology and an influential figure in the development of evolutionary anthropology, General Pitt Rivers, left his entire collection of more than 18,000 artefacts to Oxford on the condition that it was housed in a purpose-built museum.

You enter the Pitt Rivers Museum from the courtyard, leaving Darwin and the evolution of the natural world behind and entering another awe-inspiring world of man's social evolution through made objects. Added to over the years, the collection now contains nearly half a million objects crammed into display cases on three floors. On Pitt Rivers's insistence, everything is arranged according to type rather than particular cultures, so that you can see how anything, from musical instruments, jewellery and weapons to toys, baby-carriers, smoking and stimulants, has evolved over thousands of years in every corner of the globe.

Facing page: the Oxford University Museum of Natural History

PHOTOGRAPH COURTESY © OXFORD UNIVERSITY MUSEUM OF NATURAL HISTORY

Stripped for cash

As a student short of money in the Eighties, **DAEMIENNE SHEEHAN** *swapped studying for stripping. But the life of a strip-o-gram was a lot less racy than it looked...*

Some folks measure the passage of time in fine bottles of wine and others in the changing faces of their lovers. But one way I know that I am not in 1984 but in 2011 is by just how demanding stripping has gotten.

It was not always a round of filthy orgies for unlucky ladies long in the tooth and big in the back, I can assure you. Back in the early 1980s, when strip-o-grams first appeared in Toronto, Canada, the emphasis was on fun that wouldn't be out of place in a nursing home. Aged 19, I was embarked on my university career, when through a devilish cock-up in the bursar's office, my student grant and loan cheque was lost and would not be re-issued for a full nine months. I visited my mother, a woman who combined aristocratic nonchalance with an utter poverty of social connections. Descended from a long line of publicans and capricious horse-traders, this lifelong teetotaller was a great imbiber of every legal opiate going and spoke in a vague whisper gently furred with the morphine skimmings from a bottle of kaopectate. I requested a tide-me-over that she appeared to consider. 'No. You'll buy drugs,' she said inexplicably. What of the mysterious education fund mentioned throughout my childhood, I wondered. With a sudden show of life, she laughed merrily and confessed, 'I made it up to keep you going. That was spent on a shop-up years ago.' Then, seeing my stricken face, she added with a dash of pity, 'You'll find something – you've always been a worker.'

As I was quite sure nothing would turn up and the rent was due, I hit the want ads where I read: 'Earn up to $100 an hour doing strip-o-grams. Dance training appreciated.'

I had no training save for a bout of Irish dancing as a girl, but I did want to earn $100 an hour. The interview was rigorous. 'Lingerie rules are simple – no black, no white, and no bright pink. Too sexual,' the Dallas-suited female boss barked between furious puffs of her extra-long menthol. 'It's pastels only. Also, we don't do front kicks: the cus-

'Ba ba boom' went the tape, as I leapt onto the table, tearing open my wraparound skirt and top

tomer would see too much and might get the wrong idea. These are novelty strip-o-grams for retirement parties and birthdays – you get my drift?' She left me for assessment with their 'top number'

– an embittered Bob Fosse fanatic who flicked her hair over her shoulders with such alacrity that it was remarkable her fingertips were still intact.

'Do the ball and chain,' she ordered, dragging her muscular left leg towards her as she reached for the sky with her right arm and stared straight ahead with a drop-dead look. I hopped elfishly. 'Drag your foot,' she huffed. 'It's supposed to be heavy.' After more dismal attempts she flounced off to wave her arms at the dragon boss who shot me a deeply disappointed look. Then a man walked in the room. 'We'll ask my partner,' Dragon said. 'He's a man.'

The man observed me inscrutably, shrugged and said: 'Take her, the dancing might improve and the legs are already there.' They handed me a cassette of the classic ba-ba-boom bump-and-grind tune that I was to play once I had tricked strip-o-gram recipients into thinking that I had arrived for legitimate purposes.

I was thrilled and immediately went home to sew extra lace on my outfit to make it more modest, instead transforming it into an erotic clown suit. My first customer was a lawyer whose spectacles kept sliding down his nose. I pretended to be a wealthy young lady who wanted to divorce her husband for mental cruelty. 'We do need evidence of cruelty,' he said. 'But I do have evidence,' I said, bringing out the tape. 'When I was on a yacht in the Adriatic, enjoying a brief respite from that horrible man, he had a sweaty little sailor row over to deliver this – and it's, well...' Here I gasped. 'It's stuffed with obscenities.'

'Ba-ba-boom' went the tape, as I leapt onto the table, tearing open my wraparound skirt and top cleverly sourced for my new job. The lawyer turned crimson and made a dash for the glass-fronted door where his staff members were howling with laughter.

I completely panicked. What were the rules? Would I lose my job if he left the room mid-strip? Would I get paid? 'Come back!' I shouted. 'We're not done.' By the time the music finally concluded, we were both beet-red and near collapse.

Strip-o-grams got easier after that. The working class were the most generous and respectful – often I would strip for a bemused, hard-working father who had a daughter around my age. Once a family clubbed together and proudly presented me with a hefty tip, while the mother packed me home-cooked fried chicken and potato salad. Strip-o-grams picked up – I was allotted a driver who was both lecherous and tight as hell. He was mildly famous in his hometown for having 'done' Europe on a dollar a day. 'I just stayed with people the whole time,' he leered. 'You don't need to buy them anything; they like meeting you if you wear a Canadian flag.'

He wanted to see me strip. 'Why?' I countered. 'You haven't paid.'

'I want to see what happens,' he whined. 'It's boring sitting in the car waiting for you.'

He would never believe that I was a 'pretend' stripper, and whenever I left for the Rooms Where Nothing Happened, he would seethe in his overheated vehicle. I began to worry on those long rides home that he would lose his temper.

That – and my cheque, reissued in time for the summer holidays – plus a posting to a university boys' party finished my strip-o-gram days (and nights). The young men refused to believe that I was a student and, a few days later, when they saw me on the university grounds, called out of their car: 'There's the stripper!'

'Good God,' I thought. 'What if I become a somebody? No one will ever believe I never did anything.'

Ah, if only it were so for the poor girls now.

'It'd be a boring world if we were all the same...'

RANT

THE MIDDLE CLASSES are constantly finding new ways to be self-righteous. The latest crusade for the chattering classes is food fascism. You know, the sort of people who nosily open your kitchen cupboards and gasp with horror at the ready-made pasta sauce, and are absolutely finished off when they see a jar of Hellmann's mayonnaise in your fridge.

Lately, though, food fascism is mixed with moralising on climate change, and the combination is toxic. Food fascists preach to friends about how supermarkets are evil, and describe in minute detail what is in their weekly organic vegetable box, droning on about what you're allowed to eat and when, having mastered the look of self-satisfied disapproval if the wrong sort of vegetable is served at the wrong time.

At a dinner party recently, I listened with increasing boredom as two couples competed over who had the most 'carbon footprint-free' vegetable box. 'Oh no, you shouldn't use Abel & Cole,' lectured one. 'They source their tomatoes from absolutely miles away. We always use Riverford.' 'Riverford?' said the other with disdain. 'Oh, gosh, we'd never use Riverford. They once sent us cauliflower totally out of season.' 'But Abel & Cole use salad from a greenhouse, which is just deplorable.' 'Well, Riverford have a magnificent greenhouse in Norfolk which produces zero-carbon tomatoes...'

On and on they went for the entire meal: 'We should all be shunning asparagus – it's carrot season.' By the time I left, I felt like heading straight to my local kebab shop to binge on poorly sourced and unethical food and strew the leftovers around their front gardens. I'm all for people eating organic, locally sourced vegetables – I just don't want to hear people competing endlessly on the subject. And I certainly do not want to be preached at. So order your bloody vegetable box and keep quiet.

SONALI CHAPMAN

Whiteboard *jungle*

KATE SAWYER

It started with a kiss...

Well, yesterday I thought it was all over. All these years of teaching, all the energy and determination and tears and pride, and I thought I'd blown it. For a kiss.

I kissed a boy.

I'd come up the stairs to be confronted by the solidly muddy trouser-legs of one of my Year 7 tutor group. Late and panicky, I snapped at him, at which point his chin did that lovely little-boy wobble (am I making it worse for myself?) and he burst into tears.

He'd fallen off his bicycle and was filthy and shaken and thinking he was going to be told off; I had, if not broken his heart, then certainly made his day a lot worse. So I hugged him and told him everything would be all right and then he cried some more, so I kissed him. On the top of his head. He's only little. The age of one of my children. But however I pile up the rationale, I know it sounds terrible.

As soon as I realised what I'd done, I backed off in a panic, and told him to come with me. And then it gets worse. I took him to my teaching room and told him to get into my cupboard and take his trousers off. We'd already discussed the fact that he had tracksuit bottoms with him for PE, but nevertheless had anyone heard me I would have been finished.

What is this world in which we live – so full of fear of the politically correct ogres? This was a small boy, frightened and in tears. I reacted as any warm-hearted mother – woman – indeed person – would have done until recently. I remember a child of mine coming home (aged about six) and saying that Mr X was not as kind as they'd all thought because when a girl fell and

As soon as I realised what I'd done I backed off in a panic. And then it gets worse. I told him to get into my cupboard and take his trousers off

cut her knee he did not pick her up, but sent for a dinner lady to help her. Even then I knew why, and hated the idiocy of our created fear on behalf of them all – the teacher, the hurt child, my child as bemused witness. I did not think I would ever fall into such a trap.

I confessed to my Head of Year, a sensible man who has no truck with nonsense. But even he blanched. 'Where did you kiss him? Did anyone see? Did he feel the kiss? Kate, we all hug them and know we shouldn't, but kissing is wrong on so many, many levels. Whatever you do, Kate, deny the kiss.'

'I apologised to him.'
'For the kiss?'
'For hugging him.'
Very slight relief crossed his face, but then he repeated his mantra, 'Deny the kiss, Kate, deny the kiss.' He left me with these frightening words: 'We'll have to wait until the morning and see if we get a call.'

We didn't. The boy came back today without a care in the world, and certainly with no mother in his wake screaming allegations of abuse. I spent a sleepless night imagining the worst; and the worst was not actually that I was laid off on full pay for six months while my innocence of paedophilia was proved. The worst was the awareness that if one of my children came home from school and said 'Miss kissed me', I too would at first ask myself why, and doubt the teacher's intentions.

That is how thoroughly our Brave New World has corrupted me.

'You and your suicide attempts – have you seen this quarter's gas bill?'

ILLUSTRATED BY PETER BAILEY

BORE TV (See Digital Channel 356)
This week's highlights 6 – 12 December 2010

❖ THE STANSTED FILES
Monday 7pm, Bore TV

Karen and Don have booked onto a charter flight to Majorca but owing to traffic congestion on the M25 they miss their flight. Customer Care's Julie has her work cut out comforting a distraught Don who has since lost his wife in the long-stay car park. And it's Gary's first day serving in-flight drinks on the Newcastle shuttle. Can he control his shaking hand? (S) (147842)

❖ CLIMATEWATCH
EPISODE 4 OF 9
Friday 8pm, Bore TV

This week we're live from the rain gauge in Berwick-upon-Tweed. Will it top four inches? We also check in on the windsocks in Cambridge and York. Lewis Barber reports from Greenwich's National Barometer museum. Plus regular updates from our weather-vane-web-cam in Norwich [contains some strong language]. (S)(999132)

NEW SERIES

❖ DECISION
Wednesday 11pm, Bore TV

Persuaded by his partner Jenny that it is time for him to invest in a new mobile, Hamish must decide which one to choose. Communications expert Barry, an old schoolfriend, talks him though the bewildering range of alternatives. (S)(134542)

♣ WHAT AM I BID?
Friday 6:30pm, Bore TV

The team is in a disused kettle factory in Stockton and the lots include a McDonald's menu from 1994 signed by Paul Weller and a set of Victorian fish knives. But there is trouble when RSPB officials confiscate a collection of old birds' eggs [repeat]. (S) (145192)

❖ BRAINSTORM
With Roy Shears
Friday 9pm, Bore TV

It's the turn of Jim Susskind, CEO of Luton Garden Machinery Co, to call for some bright new ideas from his assembled staff. On offer: a mower with headlights for night-time use and a solar-powered hedge trimmer. Drama when Susskind loses his cool, denouncing his employees as 'a load of half-witted w***ers'. (S)(9789132)

❖ THE AGES OF STEPHEN FRY
BBC FOUR SPECIAL
Friday 9:30pm, Bore TV

What would icon Stephen Fry have thought if he had been present at some of the most iconic moments in history? What would he have said? Using interviews with leading historians, historical re-enactments and the latest CGI effects, we gain insight into these questions. This week: the Battle of Waterloo; the assassination of John F Kennedy; England's 1966 World Cup victory.
Press your red button for: the Storming of the Bastille; the October Revolution; the Great Fire of London (featuring Hugh Laurie). (S)(999132)

PICK OF THE WEEK

❖ PET SWAP
Tuesday 8pm, Bore TV

When Sybil Sweeney and her partner Daphne agreed to exchange their pet chihuahua for a week, they hadn't bargained on getting a six-foot-long python in exchange. PLUS the homesick hamster who went on hunger strike. (S)(189786)

Pearls of wisdom

P. D. JAMES

In this 2010 interview with **MELANIE McFADYEAN**, the first of a new series, the 90-year-old crime writer shared her thoughts on life, work and growing old

Photograph by Jane Bown

What do you put your longevity down to?
Genes and luck.

You have written twenty novels, and have said that the point of fiction is to know the human heart. How do you think humanity has changed in your lifetime?
It's very easy to feel that the human race has deteriorated, that we are less kind. But I don't think we've changed. People have always had the same fundamental needs – shelter, food, work, the need for love. In the city there does seem to be a great deal more anger, aggression and rudeness. There is a great feeling that money is of supreme importance, that everything is judged by commercial success. It's easy to look back through rose-tinted spectacles – society did seem gentler, bound together by common beliefs. Of course it was an England of great inequality. I went to school in Ludlow with children in rags, badly shod, clutching a hunk of bread.

What changes for the better have you seen?
Health. Despite its faults, the NHS has been of huge benefit and there have been huge advances in medical care. We live longer and we're healthier.

You have written about the 'amorphous flattening of self in the last years'. That sounds really depressing!
Growing old can be painful, the knowledge that powers are draining away. My short-term memory is dreadful, names disappear. And I was a great walker – now I don't walk more than 100 yards without sitting down. It doesn't make me angry. I am lucky to have lived so long.

As we grow old do we get wiser, and does it matter?
When you're young you believe there's some great mystery, some great central certainty, and that when you get old you'll have wisdom that will explain life. There's no great central truth. If I believe there is anything profoundly true it is what Keats described as 'the

holiness of the heart's affections' – love and the relationships between human beings. Life is very short, and it's a mixture of joy and sorrow. As Blake wrote: 'Man was made for joy and woe; / And when this we rightly know / Through the world we safely go.'

Why are you so fascinated by murder?
I have always been fascinated by death. From childhood I was aware of the shortness of life. I don't know why. Nobody died in my childhood.

Perhaps because you grew up in the shadow of the First World War?
I hadn't thought of that. I think it probably was. All my childhood I heard about the war; there was a universal grieving after the First World War which destroyed a generation of young men. My generation was determined it wouldn't happen again. And then I remember sitting around the wireless – as we called it then – in the family house in Cambridge, and Chamberlain saying Germany had not met the ultimatum to withdraw from Poland so this country was at war with Germany. Unbelievable.

Do you contemplate your own death?
Oh yes. It doesn't frighten me. When you get old you have to come to terms with death, be ready for it. Shakespeare's the one for saying things about that: 'Ripeness is all'; 'If it be now, 'tis not to come; if it be not to come, it will be now; if it be not now, yet it will come: the readiness is all. Since no man has aught of what he leaves, what is't to leave betimes?' But we shouldn't let our lives be ruled by death: what's important is living every day, rejoicing in the fact that we are alive. If you're suffering constant pain or disability you may not have that feeling, but surely if you're not, each day must be lived to the full. Let not your life be ruled by death, let not your life be ruled by the past. We can only live in the present.

Are you religious?
I'm a maverick Anglican. As I get

older I believe less of the dogma, but what I do believe I hold onto. Maybe in some way we do go on, but I don't see it in terms of harps, pearly gates and banqueting in heaven. I believe that God is love and I trust him: there was love at the beginning and there'll be love at the end.

Did you create in your detective Adam Dalgliesh a life companion?
He's a masculine me but has qualities I haven't got. I have a huge respect for him. I took trouble to create someone I would very much like and respect. I suppose he represents the type of man I could have fallen in love with had I met him – intelligent, reticent, compassionate but not sentimental. And he's a poet.

Can you cope with modern technology?
A clanging gate of incomprehension slams down. I write by hand and dictate to Joyce, my PA of 34 years: she puts it on the computer. An elderly friend was going to Yorkshire. At the station she saw a poster saying 'Silly Cyril came to the station to buy a ticket and clever Keith got it online fifty per cent cheaper.' Why should you get fifty per cent off online? I don't go online and I don't shop online. I've got a mobile phone but I don't use it. I hate it with a passion.

What about the TV remote?
Oh God!

What is your greatest source of pride?
My two children, five grandchildren and seven great-grandchildren. And the work has given me immense pleasure but I don't feel that is anything to do with me, I think it's a gift.

If you had to finish the phrase 'Life is a...' how might you do that?
Life is a... privilege.

And what message might you leave?
I am grateful for life. My life has been very full, I have been very fortunate. I could never have dreamed of it.

Evening clashes

JOHN BOWEN *is kneed in the groin, poked in the nostril and slung onto a thin blue mat*

Illustrated by Robert Geary

Writers persuade themselves into various forms of idiotic behaviour in the cause of research. I once signed up for some evening classes in self defence, run by a local College of Further Education. The course consisted of six two-hour classes, given on Wednesdays by a sergeant of police in the sports hall of a local comprehensive school. I had missed two classes, but was told I would soon catch up. No special standard was required; the course was for people of any age. I imagined my classmates. They would be vulnerable and fearful, many of them pensioners like myself, scared of being mugged or raped in ill-lit alleys by disturbed persons in woolly hats. Even in the Agricultural Midlands there would be a lot of them these days.

I arrived early. A plump young man in a sweat-shirt with 'New York Giants' on the front had arrived before me. He was pulling blue rubber mats from a corner and placing them in groups of three and four. The mats were old and thin and did not appear to offer much protection to anyone with brittle bones.

I said, 'Good evening. I'm joining the class from today. Are you the instructor?'

'Do I look like a policeman? I'm Les. Dave's the instructor. He'll be in soon. You done this kind of thing before?' I said I hadn't. 'You'll soon get used to it. What it's mostly been so far, since I'm the only man, is them throwing me about.'

He would no longer be the only man. I too would have to get used to being thrown about. 'Must be painful.'

'Boring. It's how you're supposed to deal with different sorts of attacks. I'm usually the attacker. I come at them, one at a time like, and Dave tells them what to do and then it all goes into slow motion.'

'Surely it must get quicker as they get used to it?'

'Not really. They don't want to hurt me, y'see. And they have to do it slowly to make sure they get the sequence right. It's very important, that, the order you do things. Like right or left hand. Which fingers they jab into your nostrils. Right

or left knee in the groin.'

'They knee you in the groin?'

'Very gently. So far. Drives Dave wild.'

'But what do you learn in all this?'

'Not a lot. I try to remember what they're supposed to be doing so's I could do it myself if the need arose. And sometimes I get to throw Dave about, but he doesn't really like it.'

'Doesn't like being hurt?'

'Oh, he doesn't mind being hurt. He's very tough, all muscle. He's always trying to get the women to hurt him, but they won't. No, he doesn't like being beaten. So if I do force him to the ground, first he doesn't go easy, then he'll do a back flip to show I'm not really forcing him at all. Does nothing for my confidence, that.'

I promised that if I had to put my fingers in his nostrils or knee him in the groin I would try to strike a balance between gentleness and aggression and hoped he would do the same for me. Then the rest of the class arrived with Dave, who surveyed his kingdom like a stag, head up, sniffing the air, and welcomed me to the class.

I looked at my classmates. I had been told at the FE College that there had to be ten or the class did not cover its over-heads. Perhaps there had been ten for the first lesson. There were now five women and Les. Sue and Sandra, Nicola and Rachel, Mrs Placket.

Dave started a warm-up, and we jogged round the room, first one way, then another. Mrs Placket dropped out for a while to get her breath, and remained out for the rest of the two hours, watching from the side. I had been wrong. There was no demand among the pensioners of the Agricultural Midlands for evening classes in self-defence.

Three of Dave's former students had been written up in the local paper for fighting off attackers. 'They had the ele-ment of surprise going for them: that's important. Most of these attackers, they don't expect confrontation. Show a bit of a fight and they run away.' Sue and Sandra, Nicola and Rachel, even Les, we didn't believe it. 'Most' is not 'all'. What about those attackers who prefer a bit of fighting back, find it a sauce to appetite? But we did not speak our thoughts.

'Trouble with you ladies, you think you're weak.' The women nodded. 'Don't know your own capacities. A lady's handbag is full of bits and pieces, mostly weapons, if you think of it. Nicola, what do you carry in your handbag when you go out?' He was in full flood and did not wait for her to answer. 'Nail scissors.'

My mouth opened. No woman I know carries nail scissors in her handbag. But the first rule of research is not to contra-dict. My mouth closed. Dave said, 'You don't need a CS canister if you've got a bottle of hair-spray. Aim for the eyes.' Hair-spray! Was Dave married? 'Even a biro, it's got a sharp end. I know one lady let a man into the house and he turned nasty. She took a biro from the sideboard and jabbed the point into the side of his neck. Went in two inches. You've got to become wild animals if necessary.'

But we were not wild animals.

The class developed into a series of exercises, each with its ordained sequence of action and reaction. It was what I imag-ined choreography to be like – movements to be learned by heart and performed me-ticulously on cue – but they all seemed to involve two people, and could one rely on one's attacker to know his part? 'Let your body-weight do the work. Offer him your weak side. He grabs it – grab her arm, Les – then you can use your strong side. Now, there's a nerve on the inside of that leg,

'We're expecting property prices to rise as the available land melts...'

exquisitely painful if you can find it with a well-placed heel or toe. Don't *look* where you're about to kick, Rachel. Never look. First because it takes time and second be-cause it tells him what you're going to do.'

Rachel looked away from the direction she was about to kick and missed Les's leg altogether, to his relief. 'We'll assume the kick, Rachel. We'll do it again in a minute and get it right. Now sweep his feet from under him.' With some co-operation from Les, Rachel swept his feet from under him and he fell slowly like an ancient building

'That's right, John,' said Dave the instructor. 'Fold his arm back. Starts like a handshake. Right! Further! Dislocate his shoulder'

toppling after detonation. She stood above him, having already forgotten what she was meant to do next. 'Get your full weight on his arm once he's down.' She knelt gingerly on Les's arm. 'Your *full* weight, Rachel.' Her knees were bony. I could see that Les was actually being hurt, but Dave didn't seem to notice. 'Now order him to look the other way.' Les, trying to quicken the process, was already looking the other way. 'That's how you exert mastery. Tell him what you want him to do and see that he does it. Then jump away and run like hell.'

Rachel jumped away and ran to the other side of the sports hall. Sandra said, 'Run like hell. I can remember that bit.' Les got to his feet and rubbed his arm.

It was all like that. Dave knew nerves in almost every

part of an attacker's body which could cause pain if correctly jabbed. We offered our weak sides; we countered with our strong sides. We went through the motion of kneeing, the motion of kicking, the motion of sticking outstretched fingers into nostrils. Dave paid particular attention to me because I had missed a couple of weeks. 'That's right, John,' he said. 'Fold his arm back. Starts like a handshake. Right! Further! Dislocate his shoulder.' Les looked directly into my eyes, imploring me not to dislocate his shoulder. 'You should be able to rip that arm off. Hopefully.'

The theory seemed to be that all this knowledge would come back to us in an emergency; it would become instinctive. I did not believe it. I did not believe that, even if we could learn the choreography, so that the moves flowed easily one from the other, attacker and counter-attacker becoming partners in a dance, that this would work in reality either. The desire to hurt had to be there and was not. Not in Sandra, or Les... not even in me.

At the end of the two-hour class each of us took a turn at standing in the middle while the rest came running from the edge of the mats, one after the other in varied ways of attack. It should have been a clip from a James Bond movie, a saloon fight in a cowboy movie; it should have been like Chinese acrobats. It was none of these. It was a shambles of stop-and-start. So it went. Wednesday followed Wednesday. We lost Mrs Placket, lost Sandra and Sue; even Les dropped away. At the end only Rachel and I were left. Dave was not defeated. 'We'll carry on,' he said. 'I owe it to myself, I owe it to you. I won't say you've improved, because you haven't, but you've stuck it out. So get into opposite corners of the room, if you please, and try to come at each other like tigers.'

Dictators
I have known

Before his death in 2009, the BBC's **BRIAN BARRON** (right) looked back over thirty-one years of meeting some of the world's most unsavoury leaders

The ancient Romans knew about dictators: they gave us the word itself, the concept of a Roman magistrate who was handed absolute power in times of crisis. But the 20th century was the Age of Dictators. Mass murderers like Hitler, Stalin and Chairman Mao were followed, in my time, by lesser fry, no less grotesque in terms of their grisly deeds.

Most were military men. Since the Sixties I have lost count of the number of coups I've covered in the Middle East, Africa and Asia. The usual background was post-colonial chaos and civil war. To seize power you only needed a few tanks, the right fellow plotters and a willingness to kill.

In the roll-call of dishonour were just about all ranks – from that self-promoted Field Marshal, Idi Amin, who had opponents fed to Nile crocodiles or brained with sledgehammers, to Master Sergeant Samuel Doe, whose first act was to have the entire cabinet he'd overthrown shot in front of us by a drunken firing squad, and General Lon Nol, the inept Cambodian strongman and CIA ally, who was closeted with his astrologers while the Khmer Rouge throttled the capital, Phnom Penh.

The currency of dictators is fear. Take General Park Chung Hee, one of the founders of industrialised, modern South Korea. An interview was scheduled in the Blue House, the presidential mansion. As we waited, I noticed an ashtray

askew on a coffee table. It was wired up, containing a hidden microphone for the Korean CIA. In this police state, even the dictator was bugged. A few months later we were on holiday at a ski lodge in the Korean mountains. By chance General Park turned up for a private lunch with a dozen bodyguards in tow. Our paths came close as my family strolled across the lawn. As the President disappeared from sight, the head bodyguard rebuked two of his colleagues for allowing us to walk inadvertently close to his boss: he spat in their faces, kicked each very hard in the

shins and, as they doubled over with pain, punched each of them in the head. A couple of years later, at a shootout during a security meeting, General Park was killed by the head of his Secret Service. Shortly after that he too was executed.

In the early Seventies I shared a helicopter with General Yahya Khan, the rambunctious dictator of West and East Pakistan. This was supposedly a morale-boosting flight over the flood waters of Bengal, where 600,000 had drowned. On this and other flights that day the General was drunk, throwing beer cans out of the

The first act of the President of Liberia, Master Sergeant Samuel Doe, was to have the entire cabinet he'd overthrown shot in front of us by a drunken firing squad

Welcome to HELL
Live Folk band
every night

ROBERT THOMPSON

chopper. A couple of hours later he turned up to meet the world's media, gathered to record his reaction to the cyclone disaster. By then Yahya Khan was even worse for wear from alcohol. As he entered, the TV lights were switched on. 'Turn those bloody things out,' he bellowed. The media obliged. We all stood there in the blackness. A few months later East Pakistan seceded and became Bangladesh. Yahya Khan, having lost a war with India, quit in disgrace. He was succeeded by the suave, Oxford-educated Zulfiqar Ali Bhutto, a civilian with ruthless instincts. Mr Bhutto was a deceptive charmer, personally dispensing bottles of Black Label to keep the Western media sweet in his

Muslim state, but terrorising legitimate opponents. Eventually he was overthrown by General Zia ul Haq and sentenced to death after a dubious trial. I was finishing a documentary on the General during the final power play. Come to dinner, he said. Our host spent most of the meal analysing the MCC's batting problems. Over the saffron rice I asked him about Mr Bhutto, on death row a few hundred yards away. 'He deserves to die,' said the General. 'I have his file. It's appalling.' But surely, I countered, if you hang him you'll create a martyr – and a dynasty that could haunt Pakistan for centuries. 'No,' said the General, 'this is an evil person; I feel the hand of God on my shoulder.' A few months later Mr Bhutto, shrunken in weight, walked to the hangman's noose; a few years later General Zia, all his closest advisers and the American ambassador died when their plane inexplicably fell from the sky. Assassination, I'm sure, but exactly how isn't clear.

Few of these strongmen seemed to learn from history. Meeting President Najibullah, the KGB-trained secret-police chief who'd become dictator of Afghanistan, I wondered why he didn't save his skin by fleeing to Moscow. Instead, he was holed up in his palace as the Mujahideen rocketed Kabul from the surrounding mountains. A few months later Najibullah was outside the palace, a battered corpse dangling from a noose on a lamp-post. Master Sergeant Doe, one of the nastiest people I've shaken hands with, presided over the destruction of Liberia and, eventually, died indescribably at the hands of his enemies. At least the Romans forewarned their dictators, putting a slave in the chariot of the latest military conqueror parading in triumph to whisper constantly: 'Remember you are only a man.'

The elderly General Pinochet forgot this fact, thinking he had made himself immune from prosecution. It's true that the General gave unstinting Chilean intelligence and naval help to Britain in the Falklands war, especially when the Royal Navy was stretched almost to the limit in the South Atlantic. In fact, compared with most of the brutal bully-boys I've encountered, Pinochet was a man of accomplishment, creating the prosperous, stable Chile that stands out today in a turbulent continent. But in the heart of Santiago lie the mass graves of some of the three thousand people his soldiers and supporters killed. That too is part of the Pinochet record.

EXPAT
RACHAEL CLAYE

Beirut, Lebanon

THERE IS NO limit to Lebanese bravado when it comes to electricity.

We recently travelled north from Beirut to the thinly populated district of Hermel as guests of a friend's Uncle Ali – a middle-aged Shia who looks like Colonel Gaddafi. He had no sooner welcomed us than he took us outside to a large concrete pool under the trees where he declared we must catch our supper. He disappeared inside, returning with a broom to which he strapped a long piece of flex, bare at one end and plugged into the mains at the other.

Stand back, he ordered in the dramatic manner of a conjuror – and thrust the broom, live connection and all, into the water.

Three plump fish floated to the top.

As we feasted, I thought of my flat in West Beirut and the shell-hole in the wall, about the size of a roasting pan, through which we can see hundreds of white loops of plastic-coated wire twirling away from apartment to apartment like spaghetti. English friends who visit are amazed, and rather alarmed. Oh don't worry, we say, it's okay. But don't touch anything with bare flex sticking out of the wall. It's all live.

It's all live, and it's all illegal. In two years we haven't had a single electricity bill. The connection of the entire block, you see, doesn't officially exist.

Beirut's illegal electricity hook-ups are legendary. The state may have fallen apart during the long civil war from 1975 until 1990, but Beirutis very quickly devised their own ways of managing. One of these is unauthorised generators – there are still two or three on every street – and the other is an infinite ingenuity when it comes to rigging up connections, none of them earthed, to siphon power from the system.

Every Easter, during the annual down-pour that is the closest Lebanon ever gets to a thorough clean, someone in the southern city of Sidon is struck dead up a metal ladder in a thunder-storm while tinkering with his homemade connection.

Power cuts are frequent – and not only because of precarious wiring. From our roof terrace we can see ships queuing outside the port with fuel for the power stations north of Beirut. On one occasion the ships stayed there three nights waiting till payment arrived for the latest shipment – and indeed any number of previous shipments; Lebanon, alas, has a public debt equal to 160 per cent of its GDP.

Eventually, somebody somewhere always finds the cash – borrowed from the Saudis? Bribed by the Yanks? The theories and counter-theories are intricate – and the ships sail in. Within hours the electricity is back on, but still no bill arrives at our door.

Beirut's illegal electricity hook-ups are legendary. It's all live, and it's all illegal

And nor is one likely to. Parliament was in deadlock for more than four months after the election in the summer of 2009. Finally a new government was formed, but will it be any more effective than the last several? Our politicians are so divided that we have lived without an approved budget for five years; the prospects for reforming the state-owned power company are dim indeed. Meanwhile, the outgoing finance minister predicted that in 2010 the catastrophe that is Electricité du Liban will have costed tax-payers – if any were found – $1.6 billion.

Lebanon certainly has its charms as the fabled land between the sea and the mountains, but when it comes to the daily business of making stuff work, it seems that the man with the electrified broom is king.

It's something to think about before we head out for our evening swim – far, you may be sure, from Uncle Ali.

'"*Physick for the Cure of thy Ague.*" When was the last time we cleared out this medicine cabinet?'

I once met...

Dr John Bodkin Adams

MARJORIE GROVES's obstetric care was not enhanced by the bedside manner and questionable ethics of the doctor who attended her delivery...

In the winter of 1943 I was expecting my first child. My husband, Shirley, was in the RNVR and we were renting a small cottage on the edge of Eastbourne. Arrangements were made for me to be delivered by the Medical Officer on the base, but he was then posted to sea and we had to find someone else. One day Shirley told me that he had found another doctor. All he knew was that he had a good reputation and looked like Mr Pickwick. Later that evening the front door opened and there he was, filling the doorway. He was not quite the jovial figure I had imagined. He was a big sombre man in a long navy overcoat with long arms and big red hands. He had a round face, rimless glasses and a brown trilby hat set squarely on his head. He had come to examine me and inspect the domestic arrangements. I was not to see him again until I went into labour.

Two weeks before the baby was due the nurse moved in with us. I had never had any sex education or antenatal classes and did not know what to expect. She was not much help. When I asked her exactly how the baby was to get out she laughed and said, 'The less you know about that, the better.'

When I went into labour the nurse gave me a dose of castor oil 'to get you moving', adding, 'you are going to have pain, lots of pain, but at the end of it you will have the baby.' The pains got worse and worse and I was relieved when Dr Adams finally arrived. He took off his coat and jacket, rolled up the sleeves of his shirt, removed his collar and donned a long red rubber apron. I was given a mask to hold over my face and lost consciousness. I awoke to the sound of the doctor looking down at me and saying, 'You've got some work to do, my girl.' I remember him inserting obstetric forceps without any explanation: I felt the most agonising pain I had ever experienced and thought I was about to die. Then, after what seemed ages, I heard the sound of my baby crying and realised it was over. She weighed 9lb 6oz.

During this ordeal my husband had been downstairs listening to my screams and praying for me. Dr Adams stitched me up roughly and left, but no sooner had he gone than the air-raid siren sounded and Shirley had to rush back to the base. The nurse, who had not allowed me to touch my new daughter, took hold of the baby and said, 'We're going to shelter under the stairs. You stay where you are. You are not allowed to move!'

She stayed with us for a fortnight and controlled my every action. She would not allow me to hold my baby and bottle-fed her in front of me even though I was bursting with milk and desperate to feed her myself. Just as she was leaving she confided, 'I'll tell you something I didn't want to say before: Dr Adams lost his last baby and said to me that whatever happened to the mother he was absolutely determined he would get the next baby out alive. I shall never take another case for Dr Bodkin Adams!'

> **'Dr Adams said to me that whatever happened to the mother he was determined he would get the next baby out alive'**

I never saw him again and had almost forgotten about him when, years later, his name and photograph were all over the papers. In 1957 Dr Adams, who was by then a rich and successful society doctor in Eastbourne, stood trial in the Old Bailey accused of the murder of an elderly patient who had left him a generous bequest in her will. He was alleged to have poisoned her with injections of heroin. Police investigations into his time as a GP revealed he had benefited in the wills of 132 elderly lady patients, inheriting large sums of money, valuable antiques and six Rolls Royces.

After a trial lasting three weeks he was found not guilty of murder, owing to doubts about the reliability of the evidence. He was convicted of prescription fraud and temporarily struck off the medical register. Four years later he was allowed to return to his practice and his adoring old ladies, who thought he had been grievously wronged.

Dr Adams lived to be 84 and a few years before he died a friend of mine came back from a holiday in Madeira saying that she had seen him in the lounge of her hotel sitting with two old ladies sharing a large box of chocolates.

Profitable Wonders
by James Le Fanu

Something to crow about

It goes without saying that all living creatures, no matter how humble, possess their own specialised instinctive forms of skill and intelligence – from the common housefly with its dot-sized brain performing miracles of acrobatics, to the Arctic tern navigating by the stars its annual 25,000 mile transglobal migration.

It is difficult to know which is the more astonishing – the salmon finding its way back from the depths of the ocean to the same small stream from which it set out, or the female parasitic ant that gains entry to a colony of its host by seizing a worker and rubbing it with brushes on her legs to transfer its scent.

But none possesses the standard hallmarks of human intelligence – an understanding of how the world works, the recognition how causes have effects and the ability to creatively anticipate the future. They don't even come close – not even our primate cousins, despite much badgering over the years by researchers intent on demonstrating their evolutionary continuity with ourselves.

They may be able to crack a nut with a stone and fish for termites with a stick, but it is one thing to know that a tool works, and quite another to know how it works. German ethologist Wolfgang Köhler was delighted that his prize chimp Sultan, after a month's training, should have learnt how to pile boxes on each other to reach an inaccessible banana. He then placed the banana just outside the cage with a stick to retrieve it in easy reach – and what did Sultan do? He first dragged one of the boxes to the spot in the cage opposite the banana and turned one side then the other towards the bars 'quite stupidly'. He then fetched more boxes and began to build a tower as if reaching up would, as before, achieve the same effect as reaching out.

They just don't get it, but – perhaps surprisingly – the common crow does. The corvid species to which they belong, along with ravens, magpies and jays, have emerged as the intellectual superstars of the non-human world, with entire university departments now devoted to investigating their powers of intentional deception, tool use, cooperative tasking and forward planning.

They possess, comments the (appropriately named) Dr Chris Bird of the Zoology Department at Cambridge, not just a generalised flexible intelligence, but an understanding of the elementary principles of physics – as illustrated by an experiment inspired by Aesop's famous fable, 'The Crow and the Pitcher', where the thirsty crow throws stones into a pitcher to raise the water level within it. 'We gave our crows a clear Perspex tube

Corvids have emerged as the intellectual superstars of the non-human world

with a little bit of water in the bottom and a worm floating on the surface that they could not reach directly,' he describes. He then placed a pile of stones nearby and sure enough, without any training, they immediately started adding them to the tube. Crucially, 'they understood the need to raise the water level by a certain amount and did not just try to reach for the worm after each stone.'

Their habit of 'caching' (concealing food to consume later) requires not just (obviously) foresight and an appreciation that grubs are more perishable than peanuts, prodigious feats of memory (with the ability to recall 30,000 different hiding places over several months) and spatial location – but the ability, necessitated by the inevitable pilfering that goes with this type of behaviour, to comprehend the intentions of others. They have to have a 'theory of mind': 'They must be observant, vigilant, sneaky, and at times dishonest,' writes crow fancier Esther Woolfson – 'and more than that, they have to anticipate their fellows are likely to be just as prone to these unfortunate tendencies as themselves.'

But this is perhaps to give the wrong impression. Corvids on close acquaintance are, by common consent, excellent company. Their human-like intelligence ensures they are a lot more fun than our (relatively speaking) dimwitted primate cousins. And all that with a 'bird brain' the size of a walnut, but without the wrinkles. Why should that be, one wonders? The standard view is that this is an example of 'convergent evolution' where, despite our very different evolutionary paths, we and corvids have 'converged' on possessing the same sort of mental processes. A likely story.

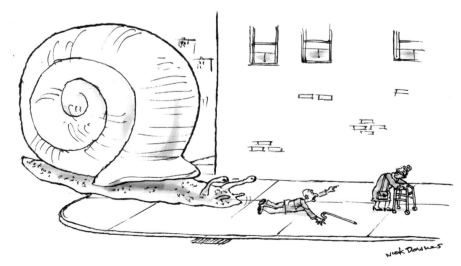

'Go on without me – save yourself!'

Hastings banter

Gangster seagulls, cheerfully anarchic fishermen and rumours of black magic – no wonder
FIONA PITT-KETHLEY *is enthusiastic about her home town*

Illustrated by Martin Honeysett

There's a rumour that Aleister Crowley, who died in Hastings, hated the town so much that he put a curse on it. It's said that no one who was born there can leave the town successfully. They keep trying but are trapped like the Prisoner in Portmeirion, or yo-yo back to the sea like lemmings. In the last few years Hastings has suffered a bad press. Apparently it once had the highest suicide rate in the south of England for young adult males.

Personally, I rather like the pettiness of local Hastings stories. I enjoyed it when someone from a coven put a curse on an amateur production of *Chu Chin Chow*, or when the world's most inept thief left his jacket behind in a changing room, complete with his name and address, after a bout of shoplifting in Debenham's.

Perhaps it's only people in their twenties and thirties who hate Hastings. It may actually be a very good place to live for those who are either much younger or older. The old reach remarkable ages. The previous owner of my house lasted to 97 and was still gardening a bit, according to

what I've heard. One of my mother's neighbours is about that age too and still very compos mentis – well, I like to think so, as he flirts with me when I pass his house.

At the other end of the spectrum, when my son Alexander was young, he loved life here. Where the Old Town runs into the main part of Hastings there are several amusement arcades. His favourite machine used to be the horse. He even simu-

The fishing end is my favourite area of Hastings. The fishermen have a splendidly anarchic outlook on life

lated it at home by jumping on my back, inserting 20p in my ear and whinnying madly. Then there's the beach and the countryside. I occasionally took Alexander to Fairlight, a couple of miles away. It was good to be able to run him cross-country without hanging on to his reins all the way.

Fairlight has a farm and a nudist beach and miles of countryside full of rare wild flowers. The walk runs through some of the most beautiful land in

southern England, the Hastings Country Park. Around the town the countryside is breaking through. Developers have built upon woodland and the land is trying its darnedest to return to nature. Being thrifty, I collect toadstools when they're in season. I have found fairy rings by bus stops, shaggy ink caps near the law courts, and a fine crop of puffballs outside the police station.

The fishing end is my favourite area of Hastings. I'm told that the Old Town spits you out very quickly if it doesn't like you. I must have passed some sort of test as I'm still here years after moving from nearby St Leonards. The Old Town inhabitants are a heady cocktail of fishing families and artists. The fishermen have a splendidly anarchic outlook on life. They strung up an effigy of our former MP on a trawler when she wouldn't do anything about fishing quotas. They love bending the rules at every opportunity. When a friend of mine lost her husband tragically in his forties they helped her with the complicated funeral arrangements as there was little money left in the pot. The husband had all his wishes honoured, burial at sea followed by a granite memorial under a yew in Fairlight churchyard. The stone was taken up there in the small hours with the aid of a tractor. The requisite planning consent was not obtained as the fishermen figured that once it was there the council wouldn't be able to do anything about it.

Most eccentricities are tolerated in the Old Town. When the Sea Life centre opened I saw a man walking down the road dressed as a blue shark. I presumed he was advertising the place. Some Old Towners thought otherwise: 'Another gay fancy dress party. We won't look to please him!' Actually I have been to some rather good parties in Hastings. The last one I went to had two six-foot French maids with deep voices serving canapés beside the pool and Cynthia Payne was the guest of honour.

Apart from the intriguing sexual mores of the Old Town there are also rumours of black magic. Occasionally local Christians get upset about New Age interest in the occult. One year a pub in the Old Town offered free drinks to those who turned up in appropriate fancy dress. Concerned local churchgoers held an all-night prayer vigil to counteract the evil. It must have worked because only one rubber-faced werewolf turned up for his free pint.

Most of the black magic rumours are greatly exaggerated, although the *News of the World* once managed to produce a shadowy photo of what might have been a goat in one of the local churches. They

could probably have got a lot more interesting pictures if they'd come to the annual 'Blessing of the Animals' service in All Saints. Every time I go something funny happens. I especially relished it when a balding parakeet whistled almost the whole of 'Colonel Bogey' during the Prayers. Someone even brought their iguana once, but it refused to go further than the graveyard, so the vicar blessed it outside.

The Blessing of the Animals service is part of Old Town week, a celebration that happens every August. A lot of the Old Towners open their houses and you can go over them for 30p or so. Personally I

Apart from the intriguing sexual mores of the Old Town of Hastings, there are also rumours of black magic

think it's worth 30p to go over anybody's house. Most of these are interesting architecturally. There are still quite a few Elizabethan properties, and usually they are spotlessly clean. I would never dare put my Victorian terraced pigsty up for inspection. A friend of mine who was in a bit of a mess at the time thanks to her Alsatian having had twelve puppies by a passing lurcher thought of throwing open her doors. 'They might feel so sorry for me they'd clean up,' she said.

One of the best things about Hastings is that it's still a real fishing town, not just a tourist spot. Every morning the boats go out and you can see them in action if you get up early enough. These days things are mechanised and the boats are hauled on shore by tractors. The plus for Old Towners is that you can buy exceptionally fresh fish off the beach. You take pot luck. One day it's plaice and Dover soles, another it's whiting and rock salmon. It's all so fresh that there's a very real risk of it coming back to life before it hits the pan. I once had the shocking experience of a plaice beginning to flap and pant while I was halfway through cutting its head off. It seemed kindest to finish the job. For the next few minutes I thought seriously about becoming vegan but instead opted for making a delightful meal of the best fish I've ever tasted and throwing the head to my pet seagull, Pantagruel.

Seagulls are a feature of Hastings life. You either love them or hate them. I have adopted various ones in the two places I've lived. They will take food from the hands of people they trust. It's like having an intelligent Hoover on permanent call. I only need go to the back door or a window and any unwanted food is removed immediately. I have also noticed that they don't defecate on people who feed them regularly. I have become convinced over the years that they are running a protection racket. I make sure I pay my Mafia dues.

MEMORY LANE

Every month Oldie readers take a trip down Memory Lane and describe what they were doing 40, 50, 60, 70 or 80 years ago

60 years ago I used to frequent the old Hackney Empire music hall on a Saturday night. I remember booing and throwing tomatoes at the stage during poor performances. One night the police came to arrest us but one of them recognised me as the son of a fellow policeman and he pushed me into the toilets whilst leading the others away to be charged with unruly behaviour. A good favour indeed.

I was there when the manager and usherettes came onto the stage with trays of jam doughnuts, a gift from a local bakery. They were the first shop doughnuts after the war. After a little speech about how lucky we all were they threw the doughnuts into the audience – to be met, after a moment, by a hail of doughnuts being thrown back. Before beating a hasty retreat he shouted that we were a bunch of ungrateful louts.

I was also there when an act came on comprising of a husband and wife and a lion. The woman rushed onto the stage, dressed in an apology of a leotard, pretending to be chased through the jungle by the lion. The lion was visibly reluctant and had to be pushed

Hackney Empire

onto the stage. When she pretended to swoon, the lion wandered over and stood over her. Her husband, dressed as a hunter and obviously drunk, stumbled on and pretended to whip the lion. By now the animal had started to growl and tug at the wife's leotard with his toothless jaws. After a few squeaks for help from the woman, the curtains were drawn to a chorus of boos and ribald suggestions from the audience.

The next act was Spike Milligan and his jazz band who were well received. After a while the band members were distracted by something going on behind the curtains. Milligan had a look and immediately requested they be drawn open. The audience could now see the husband drunkenly hitting the lion in a vain attempt to get it off his wife. Meanwhile the lion was trying to tear off her leotard in an attempt to get at the raw meat she had hidden beneath it to get the animal interested. The struggle was getting desperate because the meat was intended for the couple's dinner and the lion was equally determined to have it.

The audience were in an uproar. Eventually the stage hands tied a rope around the lion and started to drag it, and the woman, from the stage. Spike Milligan, seizing his chance, jumped astride the lion and was dragged off with it shouting Tally-Ho and playing 'The Post Horn Gallop' on his trumpet. It was generally considered to have been the best act seen there for a long time.

John Miles

80 years ago I was a prep school boarder and my headmaster was, I think, the most sadistic man I ever met. It was winter and the large house was very cold. The cellars were out of bounds and we seldom dared visit them, not only because of the temperature and the darkness but because of the resident rats, some free, some trying desperately to escape from the wire cages in which they had been trapped.

Periodically the headmaster would announce that our mid-morning break would be a 'rat break' and we were to assemble at the fives court to watch the sport. The cages would be placed on the concrete floor. The headmaster would then arrive with a terrier under each arm, letting them loose in the fives courts before

The headmaster's cane, thin and supple, was in constant use at my prep school

releasing the rats, who would run out wildly, shrieking as they tried to climb the sheer walls before falling back into the terriers' jaws. Within seconds the rats had been torn to pieces, blood spilling over the floors. A gardener would then clean up in readiness for afternoon games.

The headmaster's cane, thin and supple, was in constant use. For some misdemeanours the whole school, including the staff and his wife, would be summoned to the elegant ballroom to bear witness. We were grouped in an organised circle to await the head's arrival. He would call the victim to the centre of the arena,

bend him over a wooden chair and carry out the sentence – never less than six strokes.

On one occasion, surprisingly, it was my brother's turn. 'Surprisingly', because Tony was responsible and well-behaved and would later become head boy. (He was four years older than me and was killed in the RAF during the war.) I cannot remember what he had done to deserve this treatment but his name was called and he bent over the wooden chair. The headmaster raised his cane high above his head and then paused. 'Where is Baldwyn Two?' I was cowering behind my peers, eyes closed. 'Come to the front at once,' he said. I did so. 'Open your eyes and keep them open.' The sentence was carried out and my brother remained silent throughout. He was always much braver than me.

Richard Baldwyn

50 years ago I was flying an RAF Shackleton from Cyprus to Malta. Near Crete we were intercepted by a cylindrical, metal-looking object with no visible means of support or propulsion but with a ghostly red light around the nose. It was early morning, but daylight. We flew westwards at 2,000 feet, 160 knots. Our friend formatted on our port side and, whatever we did, stayed there.

Twelve of us saw it clearly. I climbed to 10,000 feet, sent a sighting report and put my radar responder to NATO emergency.

Two hours later we were intercepted by two RAF Javelin fighters who said they could see the UFO. It immediately disappeared heavenward at colossal speed. Malta radar said they lost it at 60,000 feet, going too fast for them to measure.

After landing, we all, including the fighter pilots, reported what we had seen and it became an Official Secret. I was an experienced Squadron Leader pilot, had flown with the RAF since 1940 and survived the war and other operations. This thing was real and not a fantasy. I don't think anyone on this planet then or now could produce that sort of capability.

Gordon Burgess

40 years ago [*in July 2009*] I attended The Rolling Stones free concert in Hyde Park along with thousands of other fans. Cancellation rumours were rife as Brian Jones had died two days before, and although he wasn't playing with the group by then, he was still regarded as very much a part of it.

We couldn't get near the stage – in fact we could hardly see it. Internal security for the day had been handed over to the Hell's Angels – you simply didn't argue with those guys, so we found ourselves a piece of grass and occupied it. Most people sat down and a sea of calm transcended the place as we gazed expectantly at the distant horizon, waiting … hoping. I remember the warm summer sun and the tumultuous acclaim as Jagger emerged, too far off to see, but the sound production was brilliant. He brought us to our feet and as he began reading Shelley's poem 'Adonais' [*see left*], the park fell silent. There couldn't have been a better tribute than the songs which followed.

I only discovered Jagger was wearing that white suit when I caught the news headlines later that night. However, it's the memory of being with so many people, peacefully enjoying the park, that has remained through the years.

Lynda Turner

70 years ago, when I was eight, my father noticed that I could not bend over and I was subsequently diagnosed with TB of the spine. I was transported across London in a Green Line bus converted to take stretchers to Stockwood Park, a stately home in Luton complete with massive oil paintings on the wall.

I was placed in a plaster bed, a half cast of my body from knees to the top of my head, supported on a wooden frame. The only thing between the plaster and me was a thin piece of muslin. I spent three and a half years so confined, occasionally being lifted out for a blanket bath or X-ray, or for another cast to be made.

Life went on as normal for the four years I was there. We had schooling and we did craftwork and singing. When I came home I was ahead of the children at my secondary school.

There are so many memories: shaking a piece of soap in the bowl of water brought at 6.30 to convince nurse that you had washed – which you had not; the question 'Have you been today?' and the dose of senna if you had not; beds placed daily outside in the sun, and me wearing the skimpiest g-string; hearing boys who were temporarily out of plaster sliding around the floor on a blanket when the nurses had gone to supper; fortnightly visiting on Sundays from two till five.

Eventually it was decided that I was cured and could get up. But first I was laid for an hour a day on a board, the angle of which was increased until I could be upright without being dizzy. Then I was an 'up boy' and was finally allowed home.

That was how it was then.

Charles Cooper

• See also page 18: The Sanatorium Children

RANT

TELEVISION directors are indoctrinated with the idea that 'talking heads' make the audience switch over or off. So they gave us 'walking heads'. Historians like Sharkey or Schama, archaeology buffs, travellers, nature-lovers and art historians are required to display their subjects by tramping through or all over them, shot from eccentric overhead angles or coming straight at the camera, preoccupied by whether they will reach the end of their sentence before they collide with it. Lately we have trailed the coasts of Britain with oil-skinned ramblers shouting their commentary from cliff paths into a high wind. Not long ago a tour of the world's wonders by Dan Cruickshank was rendered pointless by our getting only the briefest squints at them over his shoulder or behind his snatching gestures.

'Walking heads' are now being replaced by 'driving heads'. Scarcely five minutes of documentary pass without the reporter climbing behind the wheel to tell us where he's going next. Ageing comedians like Palin, Fry and Merton tour exotic places at the wheel of a taxi, lorry or fishing boat as if we could not believe they had moved on unless we see them doing it. Yet they never look where they're driving. Has the road ahead been specially cleared? Why do they never pass other vehicles going in the other direction? Could it be that it's only the scenery that's moving while they remain stationary?

It does not improve the commentary and it wastes a lot of time that could have been better spent seeing the world. Why not give the information in a relaxed voice-over? It all suggests that the point of the programmes is not really the places visited but the sight of the so-called celebrity visiting them. In the primitive television days people like Kenneth Clark, Dr Bronowski or AJP Taylor simply talked at the camera without moving and relied on the interest of their subject matter to hold our attention. Which it did. Their TV directors knew their place and kept out of their way.

PETER LEWIS

ILLUSTRATION BY TOM PLANT

The funeral was a dead loss

STANLEY PRICE *tried as hard as he could to arrange the send-off that his father-in-law had requested – but things didn't quite go according to plan*

Arthur, my father-in-law, lived alone in a small flat in Notting Hill, surrounded by his collection. It was not a collection of anything in particular, he just hated throwing things away. One had to fight one's way through stacks of back numbers of the *New Statesman* just to get into his living-room.

He was, after having a firmly Christian upbringing, a convinced atheist and socialist. We dreaded the time when we would have to dispose of his collection but, inevitably, that time did come.

There was no mention in his will about the disposal of this collection but, thoughtfully, he left instructions for his own disposal. His time in the Merchant Navy had obviously given him a love of the sea and years later, when he could afford it, he took annual cruises. He must have hoped that he would die on one of them because his will expressed the wish to be buried at sea.

Mr Hoades, the local undertaker, tried to be helpful. He suggested cremation and the scattering of the ashes when we next went to the seaside. We said we weren't planning a seaside holiday. Was I a fisherman, Mr Hoades asked? He had noted that I lived in North London and said Rickmansworth reservoir was a possible place 'for the scattering'.

We settled for an urn in the garden of remembrance at the crematorium. Arthur would have to forgive us. After all, it wasn't our fault that he had died between cruises. We informed Mr Hoades that the deceased was an atheist and had left instructions for a non-denominational funeral. 'No problem there,' he said.

'We normally arrange those with the Humanist Society. They do it nicely.'

It was a small and awkward funeral. My mother-in-law was there, not grieving too deeply as they had been separated and had scarcely seen each other in the previous 25 years. My sister-in-law made up the family party. There was a distinct absence of professional colleagues as Arthur had been an unhappy accountant. His real passions were for pottery and stamps so I assumed that the other dozen or so mourners were probably potters or philatelists. For my wife and

> *Maybe, I said, if there is a heaven, Arthur – fine socialist and atheist that he was – is up there having a good laugh... if that's permitted*

mother-in-law's sake, I was relieved that no mysterious, grieving women in black turned up. Looking back, I would have preferred that to what happened next.

The coffin appeared, followed a few moments later by a priest in full Anglican rig: cassock, chasuble and clutching the Book of Common Prayer. He mounted the pulpit and faced us. My wife gripped my arm. 'What's he doing here?' she hissed.

'He must be at the wrong funeral.'

'We are gathered here together to mourn the passing of Arthur...' Oh God, he wasn't at the wrong funeral. Damn that idiot undertaker.

'Man that is born of a woman hath but a short time to live...' Well, Arthur

couldn't take exception to that. I breathed a short-lived sigh of relief before the priest was addressing himself to 'God most holy, our holy and merciful saviour'. My wife was gripping my arm again and there were tears in her eyes. 'My mother's upset too. You must stop it.'

'Stop it? How?' I'd heard of people stopping marriages but never funerals. And there was another embarrassing, personal complication for me. I am Jewish, not observant, but definitely not Christian. What was a nice Jewish boy doing stopping a Christian funeral? But how would I feel if somebody mistakenly gave me one? The flat clerical voice had reached 'the sure and certain hope of the Resurrection to eternal life...' I was on my feet and heading for the pulpit. Then, out of the corner of my eye, I saw Hoades the undertaker standing at one side of the chapel. I moved over to him and whispered fiercely, 'What happened to the Humanists? You've got to stop this right away. The family's very upset.'

'Sorry. Terrible mistake,' he said, and headed for the pulpit. To attract the priest's attention he pulled on his chasuble. The priest stopped and Hoades whispered in his ear. There was a puzzled mumbling from the mourners. The priest looked flustered, then turned to us.

'I gather there's been some misunderstanding and the deceased didn't wish a Christian funeral. Obviously I can't unsay what I've said...' He gave us an awkward smile. 'But I'll do my best to finish the service.' His best consisted of continuing to read from the prayer book but simply skipping words every time he came to a mention of Almighty God or Our Lord Jesus Christ.

It was a stumbling, stuttering performance, sentences trailing away incomprehensibly. For a moment he thought he'd be all right with the Lord's Prayer but quickly realised that omitting the Our Father and anything about his kingdom coming, made a nonsense of it all. I had begun to feel sorry for the poor man but then he totally alienated me.

His voice strengthened and he read out, 'I heard a voice from heaven saying unto me, from henceforth blessed are the dead which die in the Lord...' He shut his prayer book, looked at us defiantly, and launched into, as I best remember it, 'Look, it's all very well not having any belief here on earth but afterwards in the after-life, that all Christians believe in, people like Arthur Fenton may finally see there is a God and maybe even come to believe in him.'

What a cheap, chiselling thing to suggest – a post-mortem conversion. I was too angry to speak to him afterwards. We didn't have a lot to say to Hoades either when he apologised profusely.

Afterwards I tried to console my still-very-upset wife by reminding her of her father's wry sense of humour. Maybe, I said, if there was an after-life or some sort of heaven, and her father, good socialist and atheist that he was, was up there somewhere, he would be having a good laugh. If one was able or allowed to laugh there, that is.

'You sound just like that stupid priest,' she said.

SHOPPING
ALICE PITMAN

AT LAST, THE Fred West wing of our three-bedroom semi is finally being demolished. Comprising a garage, a leaking utility room with plastic corrugated roof, a hideous khazi straight out of *Trainspotting* and a freezing cold, spider-ridden annexe erected without planning permission in the 1960s, the FW wing has been the bane of our lives ever since we moved here ten years ago. The builders have been drilling away at the concrete floor for the last two weeks – a pleasing as well as disconcerting sound, as any day now I expect one of them to knock on the door and grimly announce they have either uncovered human remains, or discovered a trapdoor in the garage leading to an underground room with a pregnant teenager in it. The previous owners, Mr and Mrs Frinton, were a curious couple by all accounts: 'They kept themselves to themselves' was the general verdict of our neighbours (although this, in my opinion, is rather sensible). Our old next-door neighbour Anne once told me how the Frintons only communicated with each other via their daughter ('Ask your father if he wants a cup of tea...' etc.) I used to think this was a fairly comical, as well as dysfunctional, way of carrying on, but now I find that Mr Shopping and I have started to do exactly the same: 'Ask your mother if I can have another lager.' 'Tell your father, "Dream on".'

I wonder if this is the way of all Surrey couples in the end, or maybe it is more sinister than that. Maybe we are more like characters from a Stephen King novel, affected by the atmosphere of a doomed house and gradually turning into the previous owners. Like the Frintons, we tend to keep ourselves to ourselves too. I can count my local friends on one hand, while Mr Shopping doesn't have any (although he likes Shirley behind the till at the local convenience store). Like my sister, another London refugee over in Saffron Walden, we tend to import our old friends.

Sometimes they come down for Sunday lunch and seem perpetually amused by our suburban existence. What they never let us forget is the fact that when we moved here the house was called Silvery Pines. Even after I took the house sign down eight years ago (mainly because there weren't any silvery pines) they still went on about it. 'How's life at Silvery Pines?' they ask, amid titters. The latest thing to set them off is my recently purchased revolving herb rack from Marks & Spencer in Guildford. For some reason this most useful kitchen accessory (£20) has had several metropolitan friends in stitches. Before that, it was the Olympic-sized trampoline in the back garden (admittedly a foolish attempt at keeping-up-with-the-children-of-the-Jones's).

As with all childhood gifts that cost the earth, the novelty of The Trampoline soon wore off, especially when my children realised that nothing beat the thrill of the next-door neighbour's even larger one with the added ingenious addition of a climbing frame, which, when you launched yourself off it onto the canvas below, made you bounce half-way to the moon. These days, the only ones who seem to like our trampoline are pigeons that use it as a lavatory and Roving Reporter John Sweeney (I don't think he uses it as a lavatory). No visit is complete without him making a beeline for this grotesque eyesore in the back garden. He'll throw off his shoes with wild abandon, leap on board and jump away quite happily for fifteen minutes at a time. I long to chuck the ruddy thing out, but Fred and Betty won't let me (mostly, I suspect, because they are so entertained by the sight of Sweeney leaping up and down on it like a 1970s Space Hopper). If I had my way I would dismantle the trampoline and throw the parts on the builder's skip under the rubble from the Fred West Wing. I doubt anyone, except perhaps Sweeney and the pigeons, will even notice it has gone.

THE PERSON YOU ARE CALLING KNOWS YOU ARE WAITING

THE OLDIE

The Oldie

The **Oldie**

FEBRUARY 2000   BRITISH BOARDCOASTING   £2.40

NOW ON THE STREETS

- I killed Macmillan's mouse ● Raymond Briggs's pin-ups
- Kenneth Griffith: My search for God ● Hoffnung was my husband ● Down to our last 18 million corncrakes

'The Oldie has one foot in the groove' COUNTRY LIFE

Lumley on Keith Richards: page 23

Come with The Oldie to the HAY FESTIVAL DETAILS INSIDE See page 55

The **Oldie**

February 2011
www.theoldie.co.uk

UNLOCKING POTENTIAL

Shirley Hughes

STEPPING OUT

SHIRLEY HUGHES ON BALLROOM DANCING **BOOKS OF THE YEAR**
ANITA THE MAN-EATER **WHO KILLED KOJAK?** SCHOOL MARM'S DRUG HORROR

£3.75   ISSUE 266

CARTOONS FILM CROSSWORDS FOOD MUSIC TRAVEL WINE SPORT BOOKS JAMES LE FANU

The **Oldie** 20 years of cover art

· ·

FREE 40-page books supplement inside!

The Oldie Review of Books

'I love *The Oldie*. I love its devil-may-care attitude' LIBBY PURVES

Osbert Lancaster page 40

The **Oldie**

ORIGIN ASSURED

December 2008
www.theoldie.co.uk

BANKERS' SOUP KITCHEN

COMFORT AND JOY

DONALD SINDEN AND BOSIE: THE TRUTH

THE MINSTER COPS CHRISTMAS QUIZ **BIBLIOTHERAPY**

£3.25   ISSUE 238

CARTOONS **BOOKS** EDWARD ENFIELD REVIEWS RAYMOND BRIGGS **MORE CARTOONS**

Join Malcolm Gluck for our end of Lent wine-tasting and feast! See page 80

'The Oldie – has one foot in the groove' COUNTRY LIFE

What is Mr Spitting Image doing now? See page 14

The **Oldie**

February 2008
www.theoldie.co.uk

BURSTING WITH FLAVOUR

UP, UP AND AWAY

John Lloyd, TV's Mr Satire   Still life with Lyons   My lonely nights with robot woman   **Machu Picchu: Dump in the clouds**

£3.25   ISSUE 227

MORE PAGES! **MORE CARTOONS!** BOOKS REVIEWS RANTS COLIN DEXTER BORE TV – REPEATS

Artist, month and year, clockwise from top left: Val George, February 2000;
Shirley Hughes, February 2011; Martin Honeysett, April 2011; Steven Appleby,
January 1999; David Stoten, January 2011; David Hensley, February 1994;
Bob Wilson, February 2008; Axel Scheffler, December 2008

The show must go on

A few years ago **DEA BIRKETT** *discovered how Britain's circuses are being killed off by politically correct local councils and misguided animal activists*

There is a war being waged in the green fields of England. It's a battle against people who wander from town to town in temporary dwellings, whose only purpose is to give us pleasure. They are considered outdated, treated as outcasts. Some people say they abuse those who travel, live and work beside them – their animals.

There are less than half-a-dozen circuses with animals left in Britain, and most of these are struggling. But these circuses are not dying a natural death; they're being killed. Circus people are denounced as animal abusers; over 200 councils have banned them from their parks. Banishment has been bolstered by violence, and circus proprietors have had incendiary devices sent to their homes. The circus people that remain are ridiculed as freaks, and their extraordinarily powerful, raw art form goes unrecognised. Unlike almost every other European country, there is no national circus school in Britain.

Circus was born in Britain. Two hundred years ago, in the centre of London, Major Philip Astley rode a horse around a sawdust ring. He discovered that if the ring was exactly 42-foot in diameter, the centrifugal forces allowed the rider to stand upon the horse's back. Now, every circus ring, anywhere in the world, is 42 feet across.

But it is in Britain – and nowhere else in Europe – that circus is being eradicated. Here the opponents of circus have won the propaganda war. Increasingly, one of the most common images of circus is not the magic, but the misery – chained elephants, incarcerated lions. Cruelty in circus should be condemned, and those responsible for it prosecuted, but to call all circus people animal abusers because of isolated incidents of cruelty is like condemning all dog owners because a man in Aberdeen once hit his Alsatian. Animal trainer Tommy Pinder, who presents eight Welsh cob ponies for Circus Harlequin, is hurt by blanket smears on his profession. 'People can't identify different circuses. They say, "The

Dea Birkett (right) worked as an elephant girl in an Italian circus. Photograph by Jenny Matthews

cruel circus". But why can't they say, "That circus is cruel, but this one isn't"? They don't realise that it's individual families who run these different businesses.'

The rivalries and generational disagreements among circus people have contributed to their tumble. They have no

It is in Britain, and nowhere else in Europe, that circus is being eradicated. Here the opponents of circus have won the propaganda war

united voice. When Animal Defenders, a militant wing of the National Anti-Vivisection Society, produced a report and video in 1998 entitled 'The Ugliest Show on Earth', claiming widespread abuse amongst circus proprietors, there was no vocal opposition. When Animal Defenders's undercover footage was played on the national news, and circuses throughout Britain were condemned, there was no dissenting voice to question the validity of the evidence. Even the Association of Circus Proprietors of Great Britain, which represents a dozen circuses, did not issue a statement in defence of their trade. Most circus people

just skulked in their caravans, hoping that the furore would blow over.

But the enemies of the art of circus are powerful Goliaths pitched against a divided, unconventional people. A multi-million-pound charity has devoted a great deal of its considerable resources to eradicating Britain's last nomads. The Royal Society for the Prevention of Cruelty to Animals calls for an outright ban on circuses with animals. Yet the same organisation's response to the Grand National in 1998, when four horses died as a result of the race, was to talk to and advise the Jockey Club. The RSPCA have no policy to outlaw horse racing; instead, they negotiate for better conditions with those responsible for the horse's welfare. Their position on circuses, however, is non-negotiable. Even a domestic dog in the ring is considered an outrage.

'It's ludicrous. They're hypocrites,' says Tommy Pinder. 'If I took my horses and – God forbid – just one died in the ring, there'd be an outcry. I'd probably be sent to prison. But because a big event like the Grand National is sponsored by the upper class and royalty and all that, nothing's said about it. But because we're a small business, we're very easy targets for the RSPCA.'

The RSPCA's efforts to close down circuses have been extensive. In 1989 they commissioned animal behaviourist Dr Marte Kiley-Worthington to write a report into the conditions of animals in circuses. 'They thought that I would support their case,' says Dr Kiley-Worthington. 'But of course, I'm a scientist, and so I went and measured everything I could think of that might give me some clue as to whether or not animals in circuses should be banned because there was no way they could have a good life.' After 3,000 hours of observation, she did not conclude that circuses are, by their nature, cruel. 'There is no more reason to ban animals in circuses than there is people having pets, having horses in stables, or gymkhanas, racing, or zoos,' she says.

But Dr Kiley-Worthington went further than saying circuses were not inevitably cruel. She found positive benefits in circus for the animals themselves. 'I think we're doing a great disservice to these animals by believing that they're robotic creatures ruled by instinct who only behave in instinctively natural ways, and that that's all they should ever do,' she says. 'All animals learn. Just like education enriches lives for humans, so it can do for animals. So they can have more exciting lives as a result of learning different things and having different experiences. And one of the things they can experience is interaction with humans in circus.' Unsurprisingly, the RSPCA declined to publish the report's full findings.

If circus disappears, it's not only the people that will become extinct. Forced off council parks to concrete sites on the edge of town, there is no grass for animals to graze. The few remaining elephants, which used to bathe in the sea and play on the beach, are no longer allowed to do so. Ironically, actions by animal rights activists have made circus animals' living conditions not better, but worse.

Circus Harlequin's proprietor, Martin Lacey, remains defiant: 'If councils really cared about animal welfare, you would have proper sites, proper facilities, proper water supply, proper electric supply, room to exercise animals. You don't create a situation where we don't have animals in circus and hope we all go away. Well, we're not going away!'

A Brief History of Telling the Time

Notes from the sofa

Written and illustrated by **RAYMOND BRIGGS**

HOWEVER DO WE ALL learn to tell the time?

Trying to help a friend's little boy who was finding it difficult, I began to think we must all be geniuses.

'Look, Tom, when the little hand is on number twelve and the big hand is on number three, it is fifteen minutes past twelve or quarter past twelve. When the big hand is on number seven, it is twenty-five to one or twelve thirty-five. When the big hand is on number six it is half-past twelve. When the big hand is on number nine it is quarter to one or twelve forty-five. Is that clear?

'Or, if you were a soldier, say, twelve midnight is nought nought point nought nought; a quarter past midnight is nought nought point one five; and quarter to twelve midnight is twenty-three point forty-five. See? Do you get it?'

'No, but I want to learn it.'

The little chap was beginning to look pink and fractious, so I thought that as he was better with words than with numbers, I would try a different approach.

'You see, Tom, instead of twelve midday you could say noon.'

'Noon? What's that?'

'Well, it's twelve o'clock midday.'

'Why?'

'Well, you know ... the *after*-noon? That's the time *after* noon.'

'What about the morning?'

'Er ... I'll look up "noon" in the OED. Hang on. Yes, here we are ... "Noon: old English *non*, the ninth hour from sunrise, i.e. approximately 3 pm". The *nona hora*, the ninth hour, see? Or, if you like, fifteen hundred ... get it?'

'No,' he said.

'Look, Tom, there's the real clock, it's quarter to eight, nearly your bedtime, or you could say nineteen forty-five, see?'

'Oh – 1945?' he said. 'That's a date, silly! We've just done it at school.'

'Well, you won't get far in history if you can't tell the time, will you? That's what history is all about – TIME!'

'I'm going to bed.'

'Okay. Goodnight, Tom. Do you know where your Mum keeps the corkscrew?'

James Anderton

DUNCAN CAMPBELL *on God's Copper*

One of the first acts in office of the Conservative Home Secretary, Theresa May, was to send a message of support to the organisers of the International Day against Homophobia and Transphobia. She assured them that her government was backing 'civil partnerships, tackling homophobic bullying wherever it occurs, changing the law regarding historic convictions for consensual gay sex and using our international influence to put pressure on countries where LGB&T [lesbian, gay, bisexual and transgender] people are persecuted.'

Blimey, some old Tories must have thought, I bet that James Anderton must be turning in his grave. It was Anderton, then Chief Constable of Greater Manchester, who in 1987 described homosexuals as 'swirling around in a cesspit of their own making', told *Woman's Own* that 'sodomy in males ought to be against the law', suggested castration for rapists and urged a return to corporal punishment so that offenders could be thrashed until 'they repent of their sins'.

Most famously, he made it clear that he felt that he was answerable to a higher authority than the Home Office. 'God works in mysterious ways,' he said. 'Given my love of God and my belief in God and Jesus Christ, I have to accept that I may well be used by God.' Thus was born 'God's Copper', a figure of mockery to some, a bastion of old-fashioned values to others. But whatever

'Spend it'

his reaction to this outward transformation of a political party that once largely shared his views, Sir James – he was knighted by the last Conservative government – will not be swirling in his grave. He has just celebrated his 79th birthday at his home in Sale, Cheshire.

Few non-fictional police officers in Britain achieve national prominence. In the Fifties we had Fabian of the Yard, the real-life detective superintendent on whom the BBC television series was based: 'In the nations' war on crime, Scotland Yard is the brains of Great Britain's man-hunting machine.' Cue police alarm bell and the screeching tyres of a Humber Hawk. In the Sixties, detectives Leonard 'Nipper' Read and Jack Slipper – Nipper and Slipper of the Yard – won names for themselves by collaring train robbers. In the Seventies, the Commissioner of the Metropolitan Police, Sir Robert Mark – who died in 2010 – cleaned out the Yard of corrupt detectives, declaring that he aspired to arrest more criminals than he employed. But there are not many more, and none who made such an impression as Anderton.

A miner's son from Wigan, he had served in the military police before joining the civilian side in 1953. Homosexual activity was then still illegal and the law only changed in 1967, even then in the face of enormous opposition; Viscount Montgomery of Alamein argued against reform in the Lords on the grounds that 'this sort of thing may be tolerated by the French but we're British – thank God', and suggested that, if the laws had to change, the age of consent should be eighty.

Anderton was far from exceptional within the police for his views; in the mid-Sixties I interviewed the former Chief Constable of Midlothian, the legendary 'Wee' Willie Merrilees, who explained that he had solved the 'homo problem' in Edinburgh in the Thirties by rounding up a hundred or so 'homos' from their favoured pubs and putting them on the Flying Scotsman to King's Cross, which he presumably reckoned was already such a cesspit that it would hardly notice.

Anderton, who led Greater Manchester police from 1976 to 1991, also made waves by what was seen as a less than supportive attitude towards his deputy, John Stalker, one of the new breed of cerebral, undeferential officers whose inquiry into allegations of a shoot-to-kill policy operated by the British army and Royal Ulster Constabulary in Northern Ireland in the Eighties was derailed in murky circumstances.

What was remarkable about Anderton was that he was prepared to make his pronouncements in public and, fatally, to cite God as his judge. He misread the times. By the Eighties, Britain was becoming a secular society. Anderton seemed like a throwback to a different era, a different century even. When he grew a beard, something that only conscientious undercover officers hoping to look like druggies did in those days, he seemed to be heading back to biblical days.

No senior officer nowadays would dream of making such remarks either to *Woman's Own* or even to a colleague over beans on toast in the canteen. I attended one police conference in the Nineties where an earnest officer explained how they had made great strides in fighting sexual prejudice in the service. They had even ensured that a male officer who had changed sex was allowed to remain employed as a constable. There was dismay in the personnel department, however, when this gesture was reported in one tabloid under the headline of 'No-knobby Bobby Keeps His Jobby.' Now police officers make up a contingent at gay rights celebratory marches.

Police pensions are generous and become index-linked at 55. As a result, the current average retirement age is 51 – and many who have left at a high rank do not feel they have to find fresh employment. Some of the big shots get security consultancies, a few do commercials: Robert Mark advertised Goodyear tyres for a while, assuring us that 'I'm convinced they're a major contribution to road safety', a phrase that now seems to call to us from an era of trouser presses and kipper ties.

Anderton, however, involved himself in the Salvation Army, did good works with young offenders and gardened. He lives on in popular culture through the song 'God's Cop', recorded some years ago by the Salford band, Happy Mondays. It is now available as a ringtone for your mobile phone, should you be so inclined.

By the Eighties, Britain was becoming a secular society and Anderton seemed like a throwback to a different era, a different century even. When he grew a beard, he seemed to be heading back to biblical days

FATTYPUFFS — K.J.Lamb

OOOH...MY FAVOURITE CHOCOLATES!

QUANTITY STREET!

QUANTITY STREET

The Song of the old cricket club bag

by Kit Wright
Illustrated by Peter Bailey

As though they found inside
An ancient batting glove an
*   ancient hand,*
Severed and mummified...

When you're down on your luck and feel
    common as muck
And degraded as deep river slime;
When you're up to your neck in a swampful of drek
And your life's without reason or rhyme;
When your heart's on its knees and each day's a disease
And Dame Fortune's a venomous hag –
    You can bet your boots
    You are in cahoots
    With the soul of the Old Club Bag!

When you're bust at the seams and you're dead
    as your dreams
And there's no credit left on your slate;
When you haven't a clue what the hell you can do
And you're right roundly rogered by Fate;
When you're all out of tune as you howl at the moon
And you ripple the raspberry rag –
    You can rest assured
    You have struck a chord
    With the soul of the Old Club Bag!

When you're wholly done in and you're ugly as sin
And the jaws of the chasm gape wide;
When you're plumb out of luck like a pig that's been stuck
Or like old Saint Sebastian's hide;
When you're dumped in a cell in the worst jail in hell
And you are its longest old lag –
    You can take it as writ
    You're the living spit
    Of the soul of the Old Club Bag!

HOUSE HUSBANDRY
with Giles Wood

In which a stricken Miss Wood tests her old Pa's patience

The word 'buck', as in 'buck up' or 'buck your ideas up', is rarely employed these days. So I was heartened to hear a village elder use it to describe a spurt in growth of the maize crop which had been sulking in the sodden ground.

'Oy see this noice weathurr's bucked the corn upabed.'

'Bucking up' is something of a forgotten concept. A new, mollycoddled generation, unused to tepid baths, chilblains and short rations, obviously needs to buck itself up. But with nothing to contrast the permacomforts of their daily lives against, bucking up would be a hard concept for them to grasp.

Besides, there is always the possibility that the young adults may not be just lazy, complacent or unmotivated. These days they may instead be suffering from one of a raft of debilitating medical conditions all of which are characterised by extreme lack of energy. These include toxoplasmosis, Lyme's disease, dengue fever, thyroid malfunction, and the very common glandular fever with which our eldest daughter has been diagnosed. Concentration is impossible to maintain and, in extreme cases, even looking at a pleasant view through a window can be too mentally exhausting for the sufferer.

Doom-mongers predict that Freya's ongoing slack attack may last for as long as eighteen months and even develop into ME if she does not rest enough. It is a malingerers' charter.

As she enters her third month of debilitation I have to resist the impulse to channel my inner Baden-Powell. Demanding that she pull herself together and buck up gets us nowhere, since she insists that any stress could set her back. 'Don't shout at me, Daddy. It's a relapsing disease.'

As she enters her third month of debilitation I have to resist the impulse to channel my inner Baden-Powell

It goes against the grain to see an invalid tucking into her food with relish, since common sense dictates that a huge appetite must denote rude health. Not so: this is yet another pitfall in our misunderstanding of this unfathomable condition.

She can summon up the feverish energy to chop a dozen of my hard-won winter onion crop to make French onion soup, yet the energy required to load the dishwasher, or even just carry her own plate towards it, mysteriously disappears on request.

She always suffered from perfectionism – this has morphed into intolerance. She has her own patients' charter of what she will and won't put up with. All rights and no responsibilities. The right to be in a smoke-free room is understandable. Less sympathy is aroused when she demands that Mahler's Ninth be turned off at the climax because it is too intense, or when she rings a bell to ask us to stop what we are doing and pass her a tissue.

Things that make her feel better often involve my impersonation of an ancient Egyptian slave. 'Stand next to me twirling your shirt in the air to stop the thunder bugs landing on my forearms,' she asks. She has also devised a new form of massage which, she claims, can aid her recovery. This requires the patient to be lying on her side while I lie horizontally adjacent on my back pummelling her back with a broadside of blows from the balls of my feet. Similar to pedalling a bicycle, this is not so much onerous as time-consuming.

One positive outcome of her condition is the chance to get to know the twenty-one-year-old patient. Quantity time is something we have in bucket-loads.

At least she is walking now. At one point she insisted on wheelchair rides along the country lanes.

It didn't go unnoticed in the village that while I parked her in a lay-by to chase after a nectar-seeking clouded yellow butterfly she could be spotted darting from the chair behind my back to grab handfuls of blackberries. Tongues wagged and have earned us the nicknames of Andy and Lou from the *Little Britain* sketches.

'What have you got planned for the autumn?' asked Mary.

'I thought I might redecorate Freya's room to cheer her up,' I answered. 'It might be the only opportunity either of us ever has to actually sit and watch paint dry.'

'Careful! You could put an eye out with that thing'

The **Oldie**'s Literary Lunches

From John Mills to PD James, **RICHARD INGRAMS** *remembers fifteen years of The Oldie's monthly Literary Lunches at Simpson's-in-the-Strand*

The *Oldie* Literary Lunches were launched at Simpson's-in-the-Strand in May 1996. Since then we have hosted them at monthly intervals and *The Oldie*'s is now the only regular Literary Lunch in London, attended by up to 150 people.

The format has remained the same throughout the fifteen years. There are three speakers, each of whom speak after lunch for ten minutes. (That, at least, is what we stipulate. Only very occasionally, as happened once with Michael Winner, do I have to point out – like Jane Austen's Mr Bennett – 'You have delighted us long enough.')

Before and after the lunch guests can have their books signed and at the same time meet and chat to the authors.

Details of the forthcoming lunches are published in the magazine. Ring 01795 592 892 to book places.

1. A festive lunch at Simpson's-in-the-Strand, 2003
2. Sir John Mortimer in 2001
3. Sir John Mills in 2000
4. Fay Weldon, Piers Brendon and Diana Athill in 2008
5. Left: Norman Tebbit in 2009; right: Tony Benn in 2010
6. Beryl Bainbridge, Richard Ingrams and Joan Bakewell in 2009
7. Barry Cryer, June Whitfield and Anna Pavord in 2009
8. Ron Moody, Chris Mullin and Colin Thubron in 2011
9. Norman Wisdom and Dickie Bird in 2002
10. P D James and Colin Dexter in 2003

Christmas with Tyrone Guthrie

Novelist **JOSEPH HONE** recalls a miserable, penny-pinching childhood that changed utterly when he was fostered and began sharing family holidays with the extraordinary cast of characters at magical, moated Annaghmakerrig

Looking back, I can be pretty certain where the turning point came, showing me where my proper future lay. It was when the famed theatre director Tyrone Guthrie, whom we called Tony, entered my life. It was at Christmas, when I was about nine, when Tony, then head of the Old Vic, arrived with his wife Judy for their annual Christmas visit to Tony's mother at the old family home, the big house of Annaghmakerrig in the north of Ireland. I was then with my Butler foster-parents, and Peggy Butler was Tony's sister, so Tony had become a sort of foster-uncle to me. I was an unhappy, difficult boy, abandoned by my real parents in London in 1939 and initially put in the care of sad, penny-pinching grandparents in Dublin, before being farmed out to the Butlers in their house in the south of Ireland. But this was the making of me in that I, with other children, came to spend summer and Christmas holidays at Annaghmakerrig, where the house became the stage set for my conversion.

Annaghmakerrig was a wonderful house, moated by lakes, remotely distant beyond its three avenues, inviolate behind fir-clad hills, boggy fields and small brackish canals; a dream kingdom, and at Christmas, once up the steps and into the big hall, with the smell of Aladdin oil lamps and candle wax, you had the first intimation of the pleasures to come. Settled and secure, the house offered both mystery and comfort – the soft-carpeted, lamp-lit rooms warmed by log fires, where pools of rose-gold light ran away into shadowy spaces, down long corridors into ghost-haunted nooks and crannies, hidden rooms and attics filled with novelties, secrets. And here we waited for the central drama of Christmas day. But the prelude was almost as good: children's parties, dumb crambo and charades in the drawing-room, getting dressed up in the hall from boxes of Victorian tat and finery, musical chairs to the tune of 'The Dashing White Sergeant' from the cabinet gramophone, and 'Oranges and Lemons' with nervous procession through a pair of arched arms, where you could be trapped on the last words of 'Here comes a candle to light you to bed, here comes a chopper to chop off – YOUR HEAD!' And later, on Christmas day in the evening, the presents piled around the tall fir tree in the study, the magic of candles and the smell of melting wax and warmed fir needles. And finally the heart-stopping moment when the brown-paper parcels could be set upon and fiercely unwrapped.

Christmas at Annaghmakerrig, with its silks of Araby, its décor of tinsel and

Tyrone Guthrie

coloured streamers, its warm perfumes of wax, fir and almond-cake icing, had a touch of *A Thousand and One Nights* about it.

And it was here, with Tony sometimes directing us in our charades, that I sensed life need not be unhappy, dull, difficult and penny-pinching, but that with Tony, in the stage setting of the house with its Victorian props and costumes, life could be 'produced' to show a much more exciting side, that in his inventive hands it could be transformed into all sorts of magic, the workaday world banished in the cause of entertainment and illusion, with Tony master of the revels, alchemist in the dross-to-gold department. Tony was a transforming influence for me.

I was an accomplished liar as a child, and often suffered punishment for this. But Tony showed me how the make-believe was entirely valid, how there was an escape from my sins and glooms through invention, fantasy, creative lies. And this was a message he repeated for me later when I knew him better, saw some of his productions and did some film scripting work for him.

Tony was six-foot-six in his socks. He towered over everything. Eyes narrowed in the smoke from a dangling cigarette, pondering some dramatic plan – anything, as I see it now, which would kick ordinary life in the pants, or celebrate it, or alter it entirely. There wasn't a moment to lose in this transformation of the mundane, nothing of life that couldn't be tinkered with, re-fashioned by his vital spirit into something unexpected, astonishing, spectacular. Everything was prey to his inventions: evenings at the soft-toned Blüthner piano in the drawing-room, when he would sing old ballads with exaggerated relish, a Thomas Moore melody or 'The Skye Boat Song'. Or just as suddenly, in his quick military way, he would go to the cabinet gramophone, wind it up, put on a record and bring forth *The Pirates of Penzance*, annotating the songs mischievously, taking different roles, counterpointing the words in a *basso profundo* or in his high tenor voice.

He was a man overcome with endless provocative schemes, of creative or sometimes destructive fever, whether directing us in our charades or leading an attack on the garden scrub, with bonfires, the whole household

'Does it contain nuts?'

commandeered, the grown-ups issued with bow-saws and choppers, we children the lesser spear-carriers as the wilderness rapidly diminished, the whole tiresome business made fun, produced as vivid spectacle, like the mob scene in *Coriolanus*. 'On! On!' he would shout, rising up suddenly from behind a bush like a jack-in-the-box, with a mock-fierce smile, urging us on, prophet-like, to smite the nettles and the brambles –

> **He towered over us, eyes narrowed in the smoke from a dangling cigarette, pondering some dramatic plan – anything, as I see it now, which would kick ordinary life in the pants**

storming the barricades of convention, in life as in theatre, setting every sort of hungry cat among the complacent pigeons, to propose and often to achieve the unlikely or the impossible. Life at Annaghmakerrig became repertory theatre for me, a cabinet of curiosities that I could pick through, finger and possess. A time of gifts indeed, and of all sorts of daily theatrical surprises.

Some years later, in my teens, I was standing with Tony in the hall of the big house after breakfast when there was a timid knocking on the huge hall door. It was a summer day, the lake a hazy blue below us. We were surprised. Visitors normally came in through the side or the back door. Tony opened the great baronial entrance and there on the steps was

a rather nervous little man in a tweed outfit, with a moustache and a pork pie hat, a fishing rod and net.

'Excuse me, Dr Guthrie,' the man said in a gentle Scots burr, 'I'm Mr McAlmond, over on holiday doing a little lake fishing in the district. I wonder if you'd be so kind as to allow me to fish your lake? I understand there are good roach and perch to be had.'

'Why certainly, Mr McAlmond. You're very welcome. Where are you from?'

'From Glasgow, Dr Guthrie.'

'Glasgow? I know it well. Splendid city. And people. I used to produce plays there.'

'Indeed. I'm afraid I'm not a theatre man. I'm in the bakery business. McAlmond's Bakeries. Soda bread, fruit cakes and the like.'

'And very nice too, I'm sure. And just as valuable as theatre. "Bread and Circuses" – that's all people really need.'

The two of them had some more chat and I had moved away before I heard a roar from Tony and peals of laughter, and a shout of 'Alec! You rogue. I would never have believed it!'

I returned and saw that the little man, minus the moustache and pork pie hat now, was Alec Guinness.

Modern life

What is ... Alternative History?

IN THE BOOKSHOP, between the lives of Hitler and the section called 'Mind, Body, Spirit', you can now find another section: 'Alternative History'.

The prime volume of Alternative History is *The Tomb of God: The Body of Jesus and the Solution to a 2000-year-old Mystery*. The claim of the book, by Richard Andrews and Paul Schellenburger, is that Jesus died but did not rise again, and was instead buried in Gaul at the village of Rennes-le-Château. Haven't we heard that name somewhere else?

Yes indeed, for the mother of all Alternative History books is *Holy Blood, Holy Grail* by Michael Baigent, Richard Leigh and Henry Lincoln (Alternative Historians often feed in packs), first published in 1982.

The story went that Jesus had a child by Mary Magdalen and their progeny later became Merovingian Kings of France, and this secret was kept by the Knights Templars. Then a secret set-up called the Priory of Sion, variously headed by Leonardo da Vinci, Isaac Newton and Jean Cocteau, took up the secret, and some priest in the 19th century at Rennes-le-Château found out and became very rich.

All this re-emerged in Dan Brown's *The Da Vinci Code* (2003), which took Alternative History to crazier heights of profitability. Yet, instead of being grateful to the novelist for paradoxically making readers accept their own fiction as fact, the authors of *Holy Blood* were not pleased and made a failed attempt to sue publisher Random House, claiming *The Da Vinci Code* 'appropriated the architecture' of their book.

Dan Brown's 2003 book *The Da Vinci Code* took Alternative History to even crazier heights of profitability

Airport bookshops are full of Alternative History variants: *The Templar Revelation*; *The Messianic Legacy*; *The Second Messiah*; *Mary Magdalen and the Holy Grail*. In them, Rennes-le-Château, a village fifty miles from Carcassonne, keeps cropping up, and is a place of Alternative Pilgrimage.

An inscription in the church there, *Terribilis est Locus Iste*, is said to mean

Is the traditional, accepted view of the life of Christ in some way incomplete?
- Is it possible Christ did not die on the cross?
- It is possible Jesus was married, a father, and that his bloodline still exists...?

Jacket blurb from *Holy Blood, Holy Grail*, by Michael Baigent, Richard Leigh & Henry Lincoln

'This place is terrible' – a cryptic indication of its importance in Alternative History. In reality it is a popular quotation from the Bible (Genesis 28:17, 'How dreadful is this place. This is none other but the house of God, and this is the gate of heaven') referring to Jacob's meeting God.

All this Alternative History goes back not to the Middle Ages but to 1956, when the French fantasist Pierre Plantard (1920–2000) became the self-styled Grand Master of the concocted Priory of Sion. Plantard, convicted of financial fraud in 1953, had in 1942 invented another order of chivalry. In 1943 he even accused the Vichy regime of being in league with French Jews. From 1962 onwards he invented links for himself with Merovingian kings of France and the usual suspects.

The Alternative History game of Chinese whispers provoked 150,000 tourists in the summer of 2004 to descend on the little village of Rennes, some carrying spades for a spot of Alternative Archeaeology and treasure-hunting: the Abbé Saunière of Rennes-le-Château is said to have suddenly become rich in the 1880s – perhaps by stumbling across buried treasure or by finding parchments that 'proved' Jesus's affair with Mary Magdalen, enabling him to 'blackmail the Vatican'.

The story of parchments and buried treasure can be traced as far back as 1955, when a local restaurateur who owned a property that was once Saunière's was looking for publicity. A document written by a friend of Plantard's, supposedly transcribing the parchments, was deposited in the Bibliothèque Nationale in 1964. A fact sometimes educed in support of its reliability.

The truth seems to be that Saunière made a few thousand francs by accepting money for Masses that he never said and was suspended from the priesthood as a consequence. However, the books documenting this are in French, and therefore unreadable to most of the American market. They prefer Alternative History.

CHRISTOPER HOWSE

Olden life

What were...
Acorn and Gulliver?

TELEPHONE NUMBERS are always growing longer, to the point that no one can remember more than two. But until forty years ago it was easy to remember a dozen or two for the simple reason that telephone exchanges had names. I can still effortlessly summon up numbers from the 1950s – such as my girlfriend's. It was Primrose 3254, for which you dialled PRI followed by the four digits.

I could go on. Everyone knew that Scotland Yard answered to WHItehall 1212 which they urged you to call if you needed them. The BBC was LANgham 4468, though they didn't keep urging you to call them as they do now. (This was radio at Broadcasting House – the lonely pioneers of television were stationed at downmarket SHEpherd's Bush.)

Exchange names which were not merely geographical had standing and character. Some identified the likely calling of their subscribers. Lawyers were to be found at TEMple Bar, expensive doctors at WELbeck, clerics at ABBey, stockbrokers (I presume) at MINcing Lane and the Lord Mayor, naturally, at MANsion House. A posh telephone number conferred immediate status – MAYfair, GROsvenor, BELgravia. I once enjoyed the kudos of an AMBassador number although I had little in common with my neighbouring diplomats.

You might have supposed that MONarch was reserved for the Queen. Not so. Buckingham Palace was a mere VICtoria number while MONarch, in my old address book, meant John Betjeman at his quaint City quarters beside St Bartholomew the Great.

A high point in the post-war act of comedian Terry-Thomas was his description of being shouted at as a conscript on the parade ground: 'A ghastly red-faced little man came up and shouted NUMBAH! Naturally I replied SLOane

4701.' Ah! The days of real Sloanes!

While the artist colony clustered in FLAxman, the sculptural alias of Chelsea, an intriguing mixture of eccentrics like Jonathan Miller, Alan Bennett and George Melly were located at satirically named GULliver.

E–K: the other City Pink'un

The curious thing was how people came to suit their telephone exchanges, or vice versa, by some mysterious process of osmosis. You felt you could tell a PROspect from a WAXlow. But then the world was smaller. All London private and commercial numbers fitted into four directories, A–D, E–K, L–R, S–Z, in yellow, pink, pale green and blue.

It was hard to see the connection between KEAts and Enfield, DRYden and Kingsbury, WORdsworth and Kenton...

Until 1967, when all-figure numbering spoiled the fun, there were two hundred named exchanges on the London network. Some of them dated back to the nineteenth century. AVEnue, for example, was up and running in the City in the 1880s, along with the enigmatic HOP, which would get you Guy's Hospital.

As more exchanges were needed, names were chosen by the Naming Committee (Exchanges) at GPO headquarters. As time went by, they had their work cut out to find three-letter combinations that had not been used already.

The committee had an obvious naval slant. One member, probably a retired Rear Admiral, had lobbied for great sea-dogs of history – RODney, CUNningham, HOWard, FRObisher – but they wouldn't let him have NELson because they already had TRAfalgar. There was a strong literary group who had got no fewer than ten great authors into the list, although they were awarded to unlikely places. BYRon was allocated to Harrow because he went to school there, but it is hard to see the connection

between KEAts and Enfield, ARNold and Wembley, DRYden and Kingsbury or WORdsworth and Kenton – perhaps they were intended as a consolation for having to live in such places. DICkens, MACaulay, KIPling, SCOtt (and IVAnhoe) were all there but not, surprisingly, SHAkespeare. MILton had been excluded by MILl Hill.

The committee all agreed on one thing – their love of nature. Even an area as bleak as Acton could be rusticated with the name ACOrn. They awarded a BLUebell to go with PRImrose, JUNiper and LABurnum. No matter how urban they were, charming vistas were conjured up by LARkswood and MEAdway, MOUntview and IVYdale, SUNnyhill and (broad, sunlit) UPLands.

All these pleasant *aide-mémoires* were swept away in the avalanche of numerals in the late Sixties. Of course they said the new 01 prefix would see out the century and of course they were wrong. The same happened to the 071 and 081 prefixes. Now the 0207 and 0208 codes are running out of steam and soon will be made longer still. Telephoning will seem even more impersonal than it was when you had names you could fit to faces, instead of numbers. Already there are days when I cannot remember my own.

PETER LEWIS

'Can't you just not believe in God and leave it at that?'

Contempt of court

In our magistrates courts, the personnel are rude, the facilities poor and the cells uncomfortable – making life very trying for offenders like **WILFRED DE'ATH**

The first time I appeared in a magistrates court was in October 1990 at Chipping Norton, Oxfordshire. The court had no custody suite, so I was held for some hours in a kind of broom cupboard while the other cases were heard. The magistrate, a local dentist's wife, was totally inarticulate and had to be told what to say by the clerk of the court. (She sent me to the old Oxford prison, now closed, for seven days.)

Things got a little better in Banbury, a more sophisticated setup, the following week, but not much. This time, the presiding beak was a local estate agent (they often become magistrates for some reason) who granted the police 72 hours to question me about a single hotel offence. (This is the time they are allowed to question a mass-murderer.) I began to think, as I have often thought since, that in a magistrates court the dice might be a shade loaded in favour of the prosecution...

In Oxford, in an even more sophisticated court where I appeared in 1991,

the Chairman, an Oxford don, turned out to be an old drinking companion of mine, so naturally he had to stand down. The two terrified 'book-ends', the lady magistrates on either side of him, were so nervous at the prospect of deciding my fate that they sent the matter (impersonating a police officer, which I had done in an Oxford pub as a joke) up to the Crown Court for sentencing. That meant I had to hang around the university city

In the criminal justice system, the further you are from London, the worse you are treated

for four months before being given a suspended sentence by Judge Crawford, Head of the Oxford and Midland Circuit, and another pair of alarmed lady 'book-ends' who were sitting with him.

Broadly speaking, in the criminal justice system, the further you are from

London, the worse treatment you get. In Portsmouth in 1992 I was kept in one of a series of iron cages beneath the magistrates court which had been constructed to hold drunken sailors and other criminals during the Napoleonic Wars. I got a message to a friend of mine, David Stancliffe, the Provost of Portsmouth Cathedral, later Bishop of Salisbury, and asked him to send me a pair of shoes, since the police had managed to lose mine. His charming wife Sarah brought them along and was horrified by the conditions in which I was being held, together with several other unfortunates. She promised to ask David to protest about them, but – to the best of my knowledge – he never did.

In Exeter in 1993, I appeared in front of the wife of the local Tory MP; she was wearing the traditional woman magistrate's large, flowery hat. (The men always sport half-moon spectacles, I've noticed.) She told me in a plummy voice that she was sending me to prison for four months on the grounds that I had committed a 'deliberate' offence. As if such an offence (an unpaid hotel bill) could be anything other than deliberate.

In Salisbury in 1995, I stood in the dock in the very court used by Judge Jeffreys to send people to the gallows. It was not a good omen. The vindictive woman magistrate, a local busybody who had somehow or other got herself made a JP, told me that she didn't believe in 'community' sentencing (probation or community service) for hardened criminals like myself, but only in imprisonment. So I got sent down again...

All courts are meant to be 'people's courts', but in reality they are run on strictly philistine lines by the Lord Chancellor's Department. The ushers are generally sour and disagreeable, and the clerks of the court unspeakably obtuse and stupid. Only rarely are there any facilities in magistrates courts – toilets, refreshment areas, nappy-changing arrangements – which might make them user-friendly. You hang around for hours in an infinitely depressing environment, along with some of the dregs of society, and are then sent to prison or made to pay a hefty fine to keep the Lord Chancellor's Department afloat. (The solicitors and barristers give themselves excellent facilities, of course.)

I am sorry to sound bitter, and I have to admit that, just occasionally, it *does* go my way. In Eastbourne in 1996, I was given a conditional discharge for shoplifting by a very nice lady magistrate. Appearing in the same court a year later for breaching a Probation Order, I was offered the choice of a £25 fine or staying in the precincts of the court until the end of business. Since it was a Saturday morning, when business finishes at 1 pm, and since my case was heard at 12.45, it was not a hard decision, and I felt I'd got off lightly for once.

The only other civilised court I know outside London and Oxford is, unexpectedly, Dorchester, where I appeared once in a very pleasant, modern committee room. The magistrate, however, was of the old school, as one might have known. A pompous little man (an estate agent, again) he declined to accept my excuse for FTA (Failure to Appear at an earlier hearing) that I had not been able to afford the £58 day-return rail fare. Was I expected to walk, or hitch-hike? He was also livid that I refused to co-operate with a psychiatric report on the grounds that I found the person writing it to be a congenital idiot. So he gave me six months. Whatever became of the notion of the people's court?

Voices from the grave

Every month Oldie readers send in extracts and quotes from long-ago published books which still have a quite uncanny relevance today...

'In our modern system of civilisation, celebrity (no matter of what kind) is the lever that will move everything.'
From *The Moonstone* by Wilkie Collins (1868)
Spotted by Barbara Harper Nelson

'People talk a lot about the team spirit and let the best side win, but if you was to sit in this bar and listen to what goes on, it's all spite and jealousy, or else it's how to scrape up enough money to entice away some other team's centre-forward, or it's complaints about favouritism or wrong decisions, or something that leaves a nasty taste in the mouth. The game's not what it was when I was a lad. Too much commercialism, and enough back-biting to stock an old maids' tea-party.'
From 'A Shot at Goal' by Dorothy L Sayers (1939)
Spotted by Jack Critchlow

'The orders were no longer to be carried out by the old-fashioned type of policeman, the traditional "flatties" such as Aristide Fumel, some of whom didn't know how to spell. Now that it was nearly all paperwork, what was to be done with such men, who had learnt their job in the streets? ... Now they had to sit for exams and obtain certificates at every step

of their career, and when he needed to organise a raid, Superintendent Maigret had nobody to rely on except a few survivors of his old team.'
From *Maigret and the Lazy Burglar* by Georges Simenon (1961)

'Before the advent of television, opportunities for giving vent to emotional infantilism were relatively limited. Now, however, every set owner can take a shot of the drug which, although harmless in small doses, cumulatively, night after night, will render the most stolid citizen moronic. Television, in short, tends to set up an inflationary pressure in popular entertainment: more and more fans chase less and less talent, a vicious spiral which ends with people swooning with enchantment for less and less reason.'
From a *Daily Telegraph* editorial, September 26, 1956
Spotted by Malcolm Ross-Macdonald

'The shops were mostly small and unpretentious; a great number of them were unoccupied, with windows boarded up. On a fine corner site an extensive store was shuttered and deserted. On the facade above the windows he traced the outline letters of the sign that had been taken down, and realised that he was standing in a town that could no longer support Woolworths.'
From *Ruined City* by Nevil Shute (1938)
Spotted by Mike Fowle

The BRIGGERS

TAM DALYELL *pays tribute to the men who built the Firth of Forth Rail Bridge*

T he Firth of Forth Rail Bridge, with its three
massive cantilevers, is perhaps the greatest
single engineering achievement of the
nineteenth century. Some 4,500 men were
employed in its construction, among them
ambulance men, bricklayers, cooks, concrete-
mixers, crane-drivers, design engineers, draughtsmen, divers,
demolition gangs, electricians, fitters, foremen, gangers,
inspectors, insurance clerks, joiners, metal-testers, navvies,
overseers, painters, pattern-cutters, quarriers, riveters,
surveyors, store-keepers, stone-breakers, template-cutters,
tunnellers, unloaders, valvers, wages clerks, watchmen,
watermen and yard-workers.

I grew up five miles from the bridge, and I remember
hearing about old men who, in their teens, had worked on it as
riveters. Other trades looked down on the rivet gangs because
of the harsh and dirty conditions of their work: they were
often bent double, and the rivets had to be driven in while still
red-hot, securing the joint as they cooled. Some riveters worked
on moveable stages consisting of planks and hung from a

ALL PHOTOGRAPHS TAKEN FROM 'THE BRIGGERS: THE STORY OF THE MEN WHO BUILT THE FORTH BRIDGE' (WWW.BIRLINN.CO.UK)

'In these days of high pressure, the saving of an hour or two for thousands of struggling men every day is a point of the greatest importance and every delay is fatal to enterprise' (Wilhelm Westhofen, 1890)

winch with iron ropes: once a section had been completed, the stage was 'walked' up the tower by hydraulic jacks. On the vertical columns the riveters worked in cages protected by wire netting: each cage was deep enough to allow a sixteen-foot plate to be riveted up without using a hoist, and was attached by iron straps to the lifting girders, which crawled like caterpillars up the towers.

'While you were trying to work it out we got clamped'

Whereas the great names of the project – William Arrol, Benjamin Baker, Thomas Bach, John Fowler and Wilhelm Westhofen – are remembered and revered, the thousands who risked their lives to work on the bridge have long been forgotten. They have now been rescued from oblivion in a book which contains some truly remarkable photographs – including one of Edward, Prince of Wales, closing the last of some 6,500,000 rivets on 4th March 1890, three years after work had begun on the bridge.

As a thirty-year-old MP whose constituency covered the southern approaches to the bridge, I was invited on a tour of inspection by its resident engineer – the immediate problem being sea-bird shit in nooks and crannies which could damage the metal. My hosts kept a close eye on me, as 'we do not want to cause another by-election by your tumbling 360 feet into the Forth'. The experience made me realise what a good sense of balance and head for heights the riveters and erectors must have had as they perched ever higher and further out over the river. This memorial to forgotten heroes is fascinating and deeply moving.

- *The Briggers: The Story of the Men Who Built the Forth Bridge* by Elspeth Wills, published by Birlinn, £16.99

Facing page: constructing a cantilever bedplate
Above right: riveters at work
Above left: the bridge nearing completion

Beryl Bainbridge
21 November 1934 – 2 July 2010

RICHARD INGRAMS *and* **PAUL BAILEY** *remember the novelist Beryl Bainbridge, The Oldie's theatre critic from 1992 to 2010*

I remember how in 1991, when I was putting together a team of contributors for the launch of *The Oldie*, I mentioned at a *Private Eye* lunch that I had so far failed to find a theatre critic. 'I'll do it,' said Beryl Bainbridge with a look of eager excitement. She was in the very first issue reviewing Alan Bennett's version of *Wind in the Willows* at the National Theatre and deploring 'the potty abolition of wings, curtain, proscenium arch, footlights and dimming of the house.'

Beryl continued to review plays right up to her final illness in July 2010. She was a dear friend and will, I know, be missed by all our readers.

RICHARD INGRAMS

Left: Beryl with her daughter, the actress Rudi Davies, in 1992 – the year in which Rudi played Stella, the heroine of *An Awfully Big Adventure*, at the Liverpool Playhouse. Beryl had adapted the play from her 1989 semi-autobiographical novel and this photograph appeared in Issue 4 of *The Oldie* (April 1992), alongside Beryl's 'review' of the play.

Beryl the theatre critic

In October 1995, Beryl Bainbridge was invited by *The Oldie* to review Ronald Harwood's *Taking Sides* at the Criterion Theatre in London's Piccadilly. She decided to attend a matinée, but on her way was caught in a flash flood of rain. The umbrella she carried 'buckled under the onslaught' so she entered the foyer soaking wet. In the company of 'other huddled drowned rats', she had to wait twenty minutes before the bar opened. She bought a coffee and a bag of crisps and was told by a youngster on the staff that smoking was not allowed. She then proceeded upstairs, where she found another bar with two ashtrays and five chairs. She secured one of each but soon had to give them up, owing to the large number of elderly and disabled persons with 'fags held in trembling hands'. All this, and more, she recounts in her article before bothering to write about Harwood's play, which she thoroughly enjoyed.

Kenneth Tynan never introduced his spanking sessions with willing victims into his drama criticism, though Harold Hobson – whom, for some curious reason, Beryl rather admired – liked to remind readers that he was *au fait* with everything French. Their reviews, however eccentric, were mostly concerned with the shows and the actors.

The Bainbridge method was altogether more personal. Reviewing a revival of *Hobson's Choice*, Harold Brighouse's famous Lancashire comedy, in 1995, Beryl began her piece with the startling information that 'on Wednesdays, in the small hours' she often did a spot of dusting and furniture-arranging while watching the telly. (Was

Beryl alone among writers in preferring to do the housework at 4 am? It's an intriguing question.) On the telly that particular morning was David Lean's film of the old theatrical warhorse, starring

It wasn't in Beryl's nature – as person, novelist or reviewer – to be unkind or harshly critical. Her preference was for the language of enthusiasm

Charles Laughton and John Mills. This was very convenient because she had just seen Leo McKern as the drunken despot who is brought to heel by his daughter Maggie, who marries the shy shoemaker Willie without his permission. Beryl thought McKern's squiffy acting was more convincing than Laughton's, but she did not mention the young actor

playing Willie. Perhaps she thought he wasn't much good and omitted his name out of kindness.

It wasn't in Beryl's nature – as person, novelist or reviewer – to be unkind or harshly critical. Her preference was for the language of enthusiasm. At worst, she can sound confused or disgruntled: it's clear that Edward Albee's *Three Tall Women* struck her as pretentious, so she concentrated on the performances of Maggie Smith and Frances de la Tour instead, but Simon Gray's *Life Support* had no appeal to her at all. She deplored

his habit of telling rather than demonstrating – the very failing, in my view, that makes him a captivating diarist.

Beryl's adult life began in the theatre, and those years at the Liverpool Playhouse and Dundee Rep taught her much that she absorbed into her brilliant storytelling. The dialogue in her fiction is invariably speakable because she read it out loud to herself before finally committing it to paper. She knew and understood the element of the ridiculous that goes into being an actor – the lovely notion of being someone else, if only for a couple of hours on the stage. Her theatre reviews for *The Oldie* reflect that knowledge and understanding as well as the unique pleasure of sitting in an auditorium when the play is really the only thing.

PAUL BAILEY

Jeffrey Bernard is Unwell by Keith Waterhouse
A review by Beryl Bainbridge from *The Oldie*, September 1999

If you are thinking of going to the theatre between now and September 25th, then ignore all other productions and book at once to see *Jeffrey Bernard is Unwell* at the Old Vic. Peter O'Toole's portrayal of the late, inebriated hack is unforgettable. In my personal opinion there are only three other performances in the same category of excellence – Nicol Williamson in *Inadmissible Evidence*, Olivier in *The Entertainer*, and Spencer Tracy in the film *Inherit the Wind*. Writing this, I'm suddenly overwhelmed by a flood of memory of other actors, Claude Rains, Helen Hayes, Bette Davis, Micky Rooney, Ralph Richardson, Edward G Robinson, Paul Scofield. They were all great because, maybe only once, they were picked to enact a character that most slid into themselves, and yet, being performers, they added something else, something both real yet theatrically enlarged.

I knew Jeff Bernard, though

not well, when he had two legs and strode upright sometimes. I was seduced by his notoriety and wrote a fawning preface to a collection of his articles, although, deep down, being Northern, I disapproved of his lifestyle. It seemed to me that anyone with looks, intelligence and connections was wicked to throw it all away, and selfish not to realise the havoc he was causing, not least to his wives and daughter.

Later, when he had only one and a half legs, I got to know him better. I once wheeled him from his flat in Berwick Street to the Groucho Club and, crossing the road in heavy traffic, nearly lost him his sound leg. He fell asleep over his lunch – I admit I wasn't the most stimulating companion – and the girls at the bar said they'd see he got home safely. For some reason I posted him a video of *Little Lord Fauntleroy* and his thank-you postcard simply said 'Little Lord F... is a pompous prick.'

To return to Peter O'Toole. The thing is, he is so beautiful of facial expression, so elegant to look at, even when crawling on hands and knees, delivers

his lines with such modulated resonance, that you begin to think Jeff was a fantastic human being, a man more sinned against than sinning. This has everything to do with Ned Sherrin's inspired direction and Keith Waterhouse's brilliant script, which had an appalled audience helpless with laughter and yet by the end believing that Jeff's descent into the gutter and the grave was the stuff of great tragedy rather than a perverse wasting of talent and opportunity.

Some time ago I saw O'Toole in a Sherrin production of *Our Song*, in which every now and then he held a pause in the dialogue so long that you thought he'd dried. But he hadn't; he was simply in command of his audience. O'Toole does it again in this play. He wears a smile on his mouth, and waits. Laughton used to lick his lips, Tracy just looked sleepy, Olivier's lids flickered over dead eyes.

The supporting cast – Tim Ackroyd, Sarah Berger, Annabel Leventon, Royce Mills, playing a mixed bunch of lovers, drunks, characters and wives – is excellent, but perhaps Mills has the best lines.

What a superb evening, sad, exhilarating, truthful. Let's hope Jeff is once more sitting in the stalls bar, drinking his fifth vodka and marvelling at his own stamina.

Peter O'Toole as Jeffrey Bernard in 1999

★ **Great Bores of Today** ★

ILLUSTRATION BY HEATH

'... this is a very exciting moment for me to see one of these in such good condition you must have kept it in the box have you? you can still see the manufacturer's name on the bottom do you see here that little star that's the trademark of the Kaufman factory on the Rhine they made a lot of these and they were very popular in the Thirties all over Europe this one was originally sold in Belgium you can see from the bottom where it says Belgique I don't think I ever saw one in such perfect condition and if this ever came up in auction but I don't suppose you want to part with it you'd be looking at between fifteen and twenty pounds...'

© **Fant and Dick**

Flash photography

Cambridge's attempt at small talk withers on the vine

'The social event of the year' the invitation announced. 'Bring £50.' In these cash-strapped times £50 can buy you a great deal. Or not. For Fungus Friend, a man with a heightened sense of his own worth, £50 was the price he put on a seat at his birthday dinner. It was good value for money, he felt. After all, it was for him.

Over the years, friends, neighbours, his Uncle Barry and even his mother had become accustomed to paying for the privilege of his company. This year however, faced with a larger than average number of refuseniks and the possibility that he would lose his minimum spend deposit, Fungus Friend had been forced to spread his invitation net wider.

Among the unsuspecting new recruits were the shampooist at his hair salon, the Eastern European trainee charged with organising his 'personal waxing', and Cambridge, a theatrical type recently returned from a creative tour of South Africa and desperate to attend any gathering that didn't involve an armed guard. The meal had been economically constructed beforehand. Three courses, no choices, and wine that Fungus Friend introduced as 'experimental' but which its recipients translated as 'cheap'.

The placement had been an ad hoc affair with the result that the conversation was strained and, in some quarters, non-existent. With little or nothing in common, many struggled to get to their starters, but as the cash had been collected on the door and no one was prepared to leave before they'd had their money's worth, the disparate party soldiered on. Besides, there had been the promise of Fungus Friend singing. It was to be a first for his new girlfriend Dee Dee, and as one recidivist told her, perhaps a last.

Sandwiched between an East Coast American woman who hadn't touched a carbohydrate since 1996 and a lone male diner who had been told this was the overflow table from the main restaurant, Cambridge did his best. But things were not easy. The lone male diner's conversation consisted only of one, repetitive, question: 'Where am I?' It was a question that Cambridge felt ill-qualified to answer, not least as he had been struggling with it himself ever since arriving.

> *He had some snapshots on his mobile phone, would she be interested in seeing them? He took her lack of response as an affirmative and produced his Nokia*

To jolly things along, and in a bid to divert her attention from the bread basket, Cambridge attempted to engage his East Coast neighbour in a discussion about the merits of South Africa. The wine was good, he said, unlike the stuff in her glass. The food was excellent, if she ever intended to take up eating again, and then there was the scenery. Undeniably, it was a striking country. He had some snapshots on his mobile phone – would she be interested in seeing them? He took her lack of response as an affirmative and produced his Nokia. 'It's beautiful,' he insisted. 'Honestly, I don't think you'll have ever seen anything like it,' he added, before flipping onto the first image.

Two seconds later, a picture of his member appeared on the small screen in front of them. It was not what either of them was expecting. 'What is it?' the startled woman cried, shifting her chair away from his. Not wanting to state the obvious, but finding himself doing it anyway, Cambridge said that it was a terrible mistake. 'I can see that,' she replied, her eyes fixed on the tiny organ. 'But what's it doing on your phone? Why isn't it on your body?' Hurriedly switching the device off, he tried to mumble something about it being a visual for a nude scene, that he'd forgotten all about it, and that in the end it hadn't made the director's cut. As she was raising her eyebrows, the lone diner leant over and pleaded, one more time: 'Where am I?' His East Coast neighbour sighed and said: 'Believe me, honey, you're in a much better place than me.'

Madame Tussauds

Welcome to London's most pointless tourist destination, says **ALICE PITMAN**

One of the mysteries of the modern age, up there with crop circles and the trend for men's three-quarter-length trousers, is the continuing popularity of Madame Tussauds. Like many things that originate in France, this legendary waxworks emporium is vastly overrated. The old bat herself started out by making death masks of guillotined victims during the French Revolution. This typically Gallic practice of cashing in on people's misery and misfortune survives to this day, in what is, bizarrely, one of London's premier tourist attractions.

Those who pass its location in Marylebone Road will be familiar with the long queues of tourists in all weathers. What they may not realise is that the relentless queuing does not end even once you are inside the building (unless you had the foresight to purchase a priority access ticket for a whopping £27.50). Is it worth the long wait? Unless you enjoy shuffling along slowly from one tacky celebrity-themed area to another, the answer is a resounding no.

The journey starts at an 'exclusive A-List party', where you 'mingle and interact' with the likes of Brad Pitt, Johnny Depp, and a preponderance of current female celebs who are pretty much indistinguishable from each other (i.e. blonde and anorexic). On past a replica of Jonathan Ross's chat show studio (why?) through to 'Bollywood and Hollywood's finest', where much is made of the entirely forgettable *Incredible Hulk* and Stephen Spielberg's *Jurassic Park*. The misery continues in the interactive Sport Zone, and beyond you'll find a weirdly disparate sprinkling of famous characters past and

The misery continues in the interactive Sport Zone, and beyond you'll find a weirdly disparate sprinkling of famous characters past and present

present (Stephen Hawking, Van Gogh...)

Then it's Royals and pop and rock legends, including Michael Jackson and The Beatles, who look as much like their real-life counterparts as my dog (not good enough when you consider they have had over forty years to get them right). Inexplicably, an entire floor is devoted to Andy Warhol, an excuse to make more money by offering visitors the chance to have their photo taken in Pop Art style and printed on a soup can.

On to World Leaders, where for another £9 you can have your photo taken at the Oval Office with President Obama.

The tour ends with a naff new ride called The Spirit of London, which charts the development of the city from the reign of Elizabeth I ('Bring out yer dead!' etc.) to the present day.

Last stop, The Chamber of Horrors, where only a handful of twentieth-

Michael Jackson's waxwork: better as a candle

century criminals are left standing. Crippen was conspicuous by his absence (had they morphed him into Freddie Mercury?): DNA evidence may recently have determined that it wasn't in fact his wife under the cellar floor, but that doesn't make him innocent. And why is Dennis 'Dyno Rod' Nilsen the only murderer represented from the last fifty years, when Harold Shipman doesn't get a look in? If there is some sort of serial killers committee that decides who goes in, what are the criteria? Body count? Method? Likeability factor? Apart from the actual guillotine used to chop off Marie Antoinette's head, anything remotely interesting, like the bath George Joseph Smith used to drown his wives, Crippen's medicine box, or the letter Jack the Ripper sent to the police, has been consigned to the archives to make room for Scream, a piss-poor new attraction where 'live actors' (as opposed to dead ones), done up as lunatic inmates of a high-security prison, jump out at you as you walk through a semi-lit replica of a cell-block. Lovely.

Before the advent of photography, Madame Tussauds served a purpose in allowing people the opportunity of seeing what celebrities of the day actually looked like. But now that we are bulldozed with their images wherever we go, the whole waxwork thing strikes me as exceedingly pointless. If the dummy is an accurate likeness, then so what? For £25 you would not expect anything less. But more often than not, the likeness is merely vague, and sometimes plain awful. They'd be better off melting the lot of them down into candles.

'He can't be named for legal reasons'

OLDIE MASTERS
A guide to neglected artists
Charles Henry Slater (c.1820–c.1890)

Still Life with Bird's Nest and Primroses
Watercolour heightened with gouache, 8 x 11 inches. Signed.

NOW THAT mid-nineteenth century watercolours are in the stylistic doldrums, there is an opportunity for those who actually love the genre to pick and choose among the many bargains on offer.

Within any group there are always extremes of quality and this is particularly true among those still-life painters influenced by the great watercolour painter William Henry Hunt (1790–1864). However, careful selection can identify some beautiful examples. Look out for the care with which details, such as the eggs, nest and primroses in Slater's work shown above, are observed and painted. There should be a sense that although the props selected are conventional, the artist has realised them afresh each time. Condition, of course, can also vary widely, so look for fresh unfaded paint rather than a general, pinkish, all-over tone.

Of Hunt's followers who raced to cover the walls of affluent mid-Victorian villas, Slater, George Clare, Oliver Clare, William Cruikshank, John Hardwick, William Hough and John Sherrin all have their moments.

From Abbott and Holder, 30 Museum Street, London WC1A 1LH
Telephone: 020 7637 3981 Fax: 020 7631 0575
Email: *abbott.holder@virgin.net* Website: *www.abbottandholder.co.uk*

Mum's the word

Much has been written about the work of the Bletchley codebreakers, but less is known about the impact of secrecy on their personal lives. **SINCLAIR McKAY** *tells some of their stories*

'You had to forcibly forget about it for so many years,' says veteran Bletchley Park codebreaker Mavis Batey. 'And when you think that nearly 10,000 people worked in the various sections of Bletchley Park... but it never did get out. It's quite incredible.'

It would be an interesting proposition to put to a twittering Facebooker now. Imagine being 19 or 20 years old and being entrusted with the gravest secret that a nation at war can keep. Imagine never being able to say a word to friends or family – even your own parents – about the nature of the war work that you are engaged upon. Never being able to say a word to the colleagues that you work with on a day-to-day basis. Or even to the colleague that you have fallen in love with.

More than this: imagine that this young person, having kept the largest of all secrets, is now required by the intelligence services to keep it long after the war has ended; decades in fact. There is none of the satisfaction of telling parents, spouses, children, what they really achieved in the war. There is none of the warmth of shared memory; no chance to meet up with old colleagues, discuss the codes successfully broken, or the freezing huts in which they worked, or the relentless shifts. Or indeed the classical concerts, the elaborately staged plays, the rich social and romantic life that flowered in such a small, tight community.

And that, for decades, was the lot of thousands of people. All the young cryptographers, the undergraduates, the Wrens, the linguists, the filing clerks, the glamorous debutantes, the actresses, the novelists, a Home Secretary-to-be – all the people who worked in rigidly demarcated wooden huts in the grounds of a country house in Buckinghamshire.

Since knowledge of Bletchley Park and its work has spread, there has been much written on the staggering intellectual feats that made it so successful. Most people are vaguely aware that the work of Bletchley and its supply of intelligence, code-named Ultra, helped, in the words of Eisenhower, to shorten the war by two years. Prominent critic and essayist George Steiner went further: he stated that the work done at Bletchley was one of 'the greatest achievements of the twentieth century'.

But for some, the enforced silence – to do with the Cold War, continued cryptography efforts, and the need to obscure Britain's brilliant successes for fear of alerting hostile nations – had a poignant dimension.

Imagine that this young person, having kept the largest of all secrets, is now required by the intelligence services to keep it for decades after the war has ended

A very good example is that of John Herivel, a young mathematician who one evening had a flash of extraordinary insight in the parlour of the house in which he was billeted. This led to the 'Herivel Tip' – a new way into Enigma that very quickly helped crack countless Luftwaffe messages. By any standards, it was an achievement of immense value. One that Mr Herivel was forbidden ever to mention.

'My father died in 1951,' says Mr Herivel now. 'And of

PHOTOGRAPHS COURTESY: GETTY IMAGES/ BLETCHLEY PARK AND MAVIS BATEY

72 THE OLDIE ANNUAL 2012

course, he never heard anything about my war career. Although he knew I had been at Bletchley Park, he had no idea about what I had been doing. I was a son who had promised great things after his school career, and who then seemed, to him, to be doing nothing during the war. And this frustration spilled out. My father said: "You've never done anything!"'

The Official Secrets Act, says Mr Herivel, was so deeply impressed on everyone who signed it that even under this terrible weight of pressure, he could not imagine himself breaking it. 'I did think he perhaps was not long for this world,' Mr Herivel says, 'but out of all those people who had signed that Act, I wasn't going to be the one who broke it.'

It was not just parents. There were also children who had to be kept in the dark, as Mavis and Keith Batey – codebreakers who met and fell in love at the Park and married, like so many others – were to find. Mrs Batey's work on Italian messages in 1941 helped the Navy to victory at Cape Matapan. But as the 1940s gave way to the 50s and 60s, their children could not be told even the slightest detail.

Yet those tiny details could escape in the most surprising ways. Mrs Batey, who became a landscape historian, and still writes books today, says, for instance, that even the numerical positioning of each letter within the alphabet became ingrained. 'Some years ago, my daughter was working in the Bodleian Library "right down in J Floor". I said gosh, ten floors down, that's a long way, and she said, "How do you know J is ten floors down?" I changed the subject. Little things like that could give you away.'

Even the Park's more prominent recruits kept mum. Among them were the novelist Angus Wilson, who was noted at Bletchley for his apricot-coloured bow ties, extravagant mannerisms and the occasion when he threw himself into the lake; the film actress Dorothy Hyson, whose chinchilla coat was the source of much female envy; her paramour, the film actor Antony Quayle; and Roy Jenkins, whose aptitude for codebreaking work seemed a little limited. All kept their silences.

Some were so dedicated to keeping the secret that when one Captain Frederick Winterbotham's pioneering book on Ultra was first published in the 1970s, they would not even look at it. One such man was Walter Eytan, later to become a prominent Israeli diplomat, who had worked in Hut 4. He recalled in an essay: 'I was shocked to the point of refusing to read the book when someone showed me a copy, and to this day I feel inhibited if by chance the subject comes up.'

Meanwhile, Roy Jenkins once found himself at a party with the Honourable Sarah Baring (a debutante who worked both at Bletchley and at the Admiralty) in the 1980s, and there was a moment of amused, complicit acknowledgement. 'I'd never met Roy Jenkins before,' says Sarah Baring, 'but I knew he had been there, and I simply asked him if the initials "BP" meant anything to him and he laughed and said yes.' The topic went no further.

But for some, the secrecy has created frustrating gaps of family knowledge, as no records were kept. 'I have people writing to me saying "My husband has died, and I never knew what he did at Bletchley Park. Can you tell me?",' says Mavis Batey. 'Well, no, I'm afraid I can't – not unless they worked in my section.'

One code-breaking veteran from Scotland, a church minister, continued to tell his children that his war had consisted of his religious ministry. They knew that he had been ordained after the war, yet he absolutely would not mention Bletchley.

There's also the story of a husband and wife who, in the late 1970s, finally told each other what they had done at the Park while the husband was washing the car on a Sunday afternoon.

The author Neal Ascherson, whose sister had been a Wren at Bletchley, found her discretion both admirable and astonishing. 'That silence was very British,' he wrote. 'Nobody else could have kept it and nobody was rewarded for keeping it. We wouldn't be able to keep such silence today.'

Mavis Batey is in full agreement. 'I gave a talk to a school not long ago,' she says, 'and the one question I got asked more than any others was: how did you keep the secret? For today's generation, it seemed completely unimaginable.'

• *The Secret Life of Bletchley Park: The History of the Wartime Codebreaking Centre by the Men and Women Who Were There* by Sinclair McKay, Aurum Press, PB £9.99.
• For enquiries about Bletchley Park Museum call 01908 640 404 website: www.bletchleypark.org.uk

'This is Dorothy, my weapon of choice'

'Are you sure there isn't, Edith?'

Rage against the screen

Nearly fifty things **E S TURNER** *could do without on television*

1. Dislocation of programmes because a handful of men are playing a ball game to half-empty stands in another hemisphere.
2. Anniversaries of Bloody Sunday, Bloody Friday and bloody everything else.
3. Neighbours from Hell, car-clampers from Hell, chefs from Hell, room-designers from Hell and aircraft-stuffers from Hell.
4. Performers who shout 'Hi!' at me, wag their fingers at me, wink at me, order me not to go away, welcome me back, beg me not to have nightmares and tell me to have a safe and peaceful weekend. (Why not an adventurous or dirty one?)
5. Eighty per cent of programmes fronted by wide-mouthed, feisty Scotswomen.
6. The No 1 mandatory drama shot of the decade: men chatting shoulder-to-shoulder in a urinal.
7. Nightly delvings by masked heroes into the guts of man, woman, babe and beast, with solemn music played during major operations on hamsters.
8. Christmas Day comedy specials featuring 'humping' and masturbation.
9. Book programmes designed to put people off reading for life.
10. Consumer programmes which take up the causes of fools, cranks, whingers and compensation-hunters.
11. Late-night cultural debates in which arm-flapping witlings give tongue simultaneously, using words for which they would be arrested on the Clapham omnibus.
12. Actors and actresses who do not give a damn whether we hear the last word of the sentence.
13. Directors who do not give a damn whether we hear any dialogue at all.
14. Reporters who ask Servicemen on the brink of action, 'Are you scared?' and afterwards, 'Were you scared?'
15. News reports which bring us eye-witnesses speaking in no recognisable language.
16. Musings, soliloquies and reminiscences by car-drivers who ought to be concentrating on the road ahead.
17. News presenters who interrupt reporters with daft questions ('Is there much blood?', 'Is there any panic?', 'Who is to blame?') instead of letting them get on with it.

18. News presenters who turn up self-importantly in Paris, Washington and Moscow to cover a story the local man could do better.
19. News programmes in which men and women speak alternate sentences, josh each other and (probably) play footsie under the desk.
20. News presenters who ask reporters questions like 'What is the general feeling in Russia tonight?' and 'How will history see this, Robin?'
21. The iron rule that if the presenter calls the reporter Robin, then Robin must instantly respond by calling the presenter Michael.
22. News quiz questions designed to give a double dose of shame to those who are trying to live down bad headlines.
23. Increasingly desperate arty-crafty shots of the Bank of England and the Palace of Westminster to pad out news bulletins.
24. Shots of 'scientists' for ever dribbling liquids into trays of test tubes.
25. Shots of motorists filling their tanks with petrol whenever prices change.
26. Shots of people striding purposefully along pavements, or climbing stairs, or stroking cats before appearing on camera.
27. Close-ups of commuters' feet on way to work, varied by crotch-shots and bum-shots.
28. Police kicking down doors so that camera crews can rush in and discover villains with faces covered in shimmering patchwork, black mist or bee swarms.
29. Chefs running their fat fingers through the food, feeling it, sifting it, patting it, pressing it, poking it and positioning it on the plate.
30. Wine critics likening vintages to emulsified jock-straps, and similar.
31. Sex goddesses called from obscurity to front wildlife programmes.
32. Endless pictures of big animals gulping down little animals.
33. Endless pictures of flannelled fools playing pat-hands when wickets fall.
34. Endless pictures of millionaire footballers soliciting applause and spitting on the breeze.
35. Endless trailers of people shouting in each other's faces, or being blown up.

36. Weather forecasters who take five minutes to say Wet, Dry, Windy or Warm, and prattle about their holidays.
37. Drooling female voices which beg us not to miss spicy, adult delights to come.
38. Dramas with opening credits which still spatter the action ten minutes into the story.
39. All those closing credits to gofers, best boys and menu-wipers, as demanded by the unions.
40. Dramas in which phones keep ringing in the background, making me jump up to answer my own phone.
41. Audiences applauding *Question Time* pundits for turning up to earn their fees, before even hearing their opinions.
42. Audiences applauding the game-show competitor who has just won £100 for identifying the capital of France and £200 for knowing that a man from Denmark is called a Dane.
43. Audiences applauding show-offs who boast of breaching the Ten Commandments, the Prohibited Degrees of matrimony and any other laws of God or man, including the Highway Code.
44. Non-stop exhortations to ring hot lines, help lines, discussion lines, voting lines, get-rich-quick lines and shop-a-crook lines.
45. All programmes in which the participants wangle unnecessary flights to California to bring back sixty seconds' worth of silliness.
46. Commercials which show cars blasting along serpentine cliff-edge roads in bad visibility.
47. Motormouth hucksters licensed to proclaim at high sound levels the unbeatable price of refrigerators and washing-machines.
48. And finally... the dreaded item about the cow with false teeth or false udders which fills the 'And finally...' news slot.

Praise the Lords

BEN MALLALIEU *remembers cricket writer Alan Gibson (right), a flawed romantic and hell-fire preacher whose demons finally caught up with him*

I was staying in Bere Alston, one of those rather disappointing small towns on the edge of Dartmoor, and had gone out to buy a morning paper when I unexpectedly realised that I had been there before, although I couldn't remember when and nothing looked familiar. The sensation was strongest outside a small, entirely undistinguished nonconformist chapel, and I suddenly realised that this was where, at the age of five or six, I had heard my father's old friend Alan Gibson preach a sermon; I had probably not thought of him for years.

The chapel was locked and I couldn't go in, but it was unlikely to have changed much in the intervening half-century and more: a small bare room lined with high-backed, dark-stained wooden pews, the walls plain whitewashed plaster, definitely no pictures; that kind of chapel. Alan towered above us in his wooden pulpit, a tall, thin man with large bones and a shock of very black hair, shortly to become prematurely white.

'Why is he angry?' I whispered to my mother; he wasn't usually like that. 'Shh,' she said.

As an art form, the fire and brimstone sermon has gone out of fashion, hardly done at all and certainly not by anyone who is likely to do it well – a warning of imminent damnation inspired as much by the beauty of words as by the glory of God (possibly much the same thing). Afterwards Alan was his old self, as my father – always lavish with charm and praise – complimented him on his performance.

In his old self, Alan was much like my father, a flawed romantic more concerned with the beautiful idea than the small print. They were both talented, affable, unreliable men, with no sense of thrift and a tendency to wander, but bigger people than those you find nowadays, or so it seems looking back.

He wrote mostly about cricket and, to a lesser extent, rugby for the *Guardian* and the *Times*, and was one of the best newspaper cricket correspondents. Later,

Musing out loud on the name of a New Zealand batsman he is supposed to have said: 'Cunis, an unusual name, neither one thing nor the other!'

he became one of the Radio Three Test Match Special regulars with John Arlott, E W Swanton and Brian Johnston, and on a good day he was much the best of the four, knowledgeable and literate with a beautiful speaking voice, although becoming more eccentric as the shadows lengthened. That was in the days when it didn't seem odd to have cricket on Radio Three, much as bullfights are still reported on the Spanish arts pages.

One of the puzzling things about modern journalism is that while the newspaper space allocated to sport has increased, less and less of it is worth reading. Perhaps the time when my father and Alan were writing was, briefly, a golden age, a more leisurely, generous time when sports writers had the freedom to go off piste, particularly when writing about cricket – you could

spend all day, much of it in the bar, writing and polishing 600 or so words; often the less play the better the report. Alan would sometimes write more about the barmaid at the Bristol cricket ground or train failures at Didcot than about the game in question, a licence no longer permitted. (Perhaps it's an illusion and a good writer just appears to have all the time in the world, like a good batsman.)

On the day I heard Alan preach, we were staying in his comfortable, untidy house in Devon because he and my father had been invited to play in the benefit match of Johnny Lawrence, Somerset's soon-to-retire Yorkshire-born leg-spinner – leg spin was an under-appreciated skill, particularly in Yorkshire, where it was regarded as somewhat heretical. He was an old-fashioned professional cricketer, never giving less than his best but not considered for the England team, underpaid even by the standards of the day, and now forgotten outside the pages of *Wisden*, where the bare statistics give little indication of his artistry.

The benefit match was unfortunately a washout, and it rained for much of the holiday, although Alan's hospitality cheered it up. Fine or not, we went most days to the beach – Hope Cove or Bigbury-on-Sea, where we raced across the sands and Alan pretended that the echo from the far side of the estuary was someone shouting back. I was just young enough to be uncertain whether he was joking. At breakfast he said: 'A good post: one cheque and no bills,' a sentiment echoed by freelance writers down the ages. When the grown-ups went out for the evening, our babysitter was a very large lady called Mrs Morris. When Alan came to drive her home, he had difficulty finding the gear lever, or so he said later with much enjoyment.

Perhaps he was then at the high tide of his life, before high spirits and comradeship turned to alcoholism. He was, it was said later, troubled by a sense of having wasted his life: he took a First at Oxford without apparently ever attending a lecture, was president of the Union and could talk as fluently about Hazlitt and the Romantic poets as about cricket. He should have achieved more, although, possibly, lasting achievement should be regarded as a bonus rather than a prerequisite of a good life. And he felt guilty about his drinking and his failures as a husband and father, which, of course, only made things worse.

Alan was dropped by Test Match Special in 1975; not turning up for a live broadcast is never a good move, and sometimes when he did turn up it was an even bigger mistake. Musing out loud on the name of a New Zealand batsman, he is supposed to have said: 'Cunis, an unusual name, neither one thing nor the other!' Test Match Special was a lot duller after he went.

Demons and despair got the better of him, although not without a fight. He had spells in mental hospitals and his last years were spent in a nursing home. When I started writing this, I expected to find that he was almost entirely forgotten, like many of the talented people I knew in my childhood, but it was a delight to discover how generous his obituaries had been, even those written by people who never knew him at his best; and although his books are out of print they can still easily be found on the internet. It appears that someone has at last made a collection of his best journalism – *Of Didcot and the Demon* appeared in late 2009 – and there should be some tapes of his cricket commentaries somewhere; but there won't be any recordings of his fire and brimstone sermons.

• *Of Didcot and the Demon: The Cricketing Times of Alan Gibson*, with an introduction by Anthony Gibson, is published by Fairfield Books, £20

Samuel Beckett

When **PHOEBE WINCH** *met the great man he unlocked one of the secrets of James Joyce's most obscure work...*

IT WAS 1955, and *Waiting for Godot* was transferring from the Arts Theatre to the Criterion following good reviews by Harold Hobson and Kenneth Tynan. My father and I met Samuel Beckett for lunch. I can't remember the name of the restaurant, but it had to be near the theatre. He was staying in what we thought was a slightly seedy hotel only because it was also near the theatre. It was clear that he was not interested in his surroundings, or his comfort, or even in being in London for any reason other than seeing the play put on, and didn't intend to go anywhere other than Piccadilly.

He was instantly recognisable when he walked in – slightly hesitantly – thin, even gaunt, with the distinctive greyish crew-cut hair. He ate very sparingly, and drank little.

For some reason he spoke of Paris in the 1930s, when, as well as being close friends with James Joyce, he was also his assistant. Joyce used to dictate to Beckett. 'We were working on what became *Finnegans Wake*, and there was a knock on the door. I didn't hear it, so when Joyce said "Come in" I wrote down "Come in". I never took it out. It made as much sense as anything else. I like to imagine earnest literary students writing theses on the meaning and implications of that "Come in" in the book.'

My father asked him if he was a happy man. Beckett looked surprised at the naivety of the question. 'No, no. Why would anyone be happy?'

The curious adventures of Eileen

Professional strong woman **JOAN RHODES** *recalled the eccentric 'Eileen, the Countess', whose colourful life made her a source of endless fascination...*

ILLUSTRATIONS BY BOB GEARY

What could I do?

One day the Countess came into the café As You Like It in a shocking state. We gathered around her. I bought her a coffee and a cream slice. 'Men!' she said. 'Do I look as though I need attending to?'

She sat there, shuddering in her dustbin-found clothes, some pearls around her scrawny neck, a schoolboy's hat at a coquettish angle on her thinning hair.

'What happened?' I asked.

'Well,' she said, 'there I was, half in and half out of a lovely dustbin in the dress factory district, when I felt something near. I turned my head and there was this vile creature all undone – I tried to get out of the bin, but it wasn't easy.'

'What did you do?' I asked.

She took a deep breath. I waited. 'What could I do?'

By her expression I could see the subject was closed.

No place like home

Peter Fisk lived in Neal Street years and years ago. He was a dancer and was in the show *The Dancing Years*. Ivor Novello was the star, so you can see how long ago it was. Neal Street was then part of Covent Garden market,

mostly warehouses and storage places. The porters rushed about with their handbarrows and whistled and shouted any time Peter put his head out of the door.

He invited me in one day for dinner, which was a wonderful stew, mostly vegetables. His room was dark and gas-lit, and permeated by a strange smell. While we were eating there was a sudden movement on the top of the wardrobe, which took up the whole of one wall. Thinking it was mice, I let out a slight scream.

'What's the matter?' came from the top of the wardrobe. It was Eileen – Peter had felt sorry for her and let her sleep there.

Later he found out that she was incontinent and all his clothes were damp as a result; sadly he told her she had to go.

At the back of the building was a fire escape and on each landing was a very old lavatory and sink. Eileen moved in. 'It's ideal,' she said. 'No hot water, of course, but at least one can pee in peace!'

Fire! Fire!

I'd been on tour, and I came back to London a few months later. Walking towards Covent Garden, I heard the bells of a fire engine. There was a fire in one of the warehouses. From a top window came Eileen's voice. She was framed in an upstairs window. 'Stand aside,' she shouted, and threw out various paper bags filled with God knows what.

She sat there, shuddering in her dustbin-found clothes, some pearls around her scrawny neck

The firemen erected a ladder near the window. 'Just a moment,' she shouted. 'I've not finished with my property yet' – and she continued to throw things out. Then she noticed Peter Fisk in the crowd. 'Peter!' she cried. 'Catch my pearls, they are very valuable.' The smoke was getting quite thick by now. Out came the pearls, which smashed on the pavement and scattered all over the place. 'Move back,' said the fireman. 'We've got to get her down.' A few moments later she was carried down, fireman fashion, clutching several paper bags.

She sat on the pavement, coughing and chatting. 'Don't move,' said the fireman. 'We'll get you into an

ambulance.' 'Oh no you won't,' she said. 'Not until I've found all my pearls.'

It seems she had been squatting in an upstairs office with all her worldly goods, including the pearls which she had 'got' from a dustbin in Hatton Garden. She refused to get into the ambulance, saying she wasn't going to leave her things in the street. So Peter took her in – 'Only for the night,' he said.

Dressing for dinner

There was a scuffle in the churchyard as the police took away the half-dressed woman – who was not drunk, as many people thought. It was Eileen, the Countess, and although she protested loudly as she was taken to Bow Street and put in a cell for the night, she didn't really mind, as she would have an undisturbed rest for a change. In the morning she was up before the magistrate, who had seen her many times before. He had a sparkle in his eye as he asked her, 'What were you doing at half past seven nearly naked in a churchyard?'

'What do you think I was doing?' she replied grandly. 'I was doing what any respectable woman would be doing at 7.30 am' – a hush in the court as they waited – 'I was dressing for dinner!'

It seemed she had found an evening gown in a local dustbin and was trying it on for size. Later she sold it for half a crown.

The vanishing chauffeur

'Let me in!' shouted the Countess outside the offices of her only son.

'I'm sorry,' said the office junior. 'I have strict instructions not to.'

So she stood in the centre of the road, stopping all the traffic until her son came to the window.

'I'm desperate,' she screamed. 'How can you do this to me? I need money.' She grabbed at her tattered clothes. 'I shall undress here unless you help.' Moments passed, the cars, though half-amused, started to honk and shout. Some money was thrown at her from the window and she picked it up and departed.

Later, at the café, she announced she had come into some cash. 'Cream cakes for everyone,' she said – and now she could find a room to stay in. A few days later, with no room and not much money left, one of the Covent Garden porters said he had a van she could buy cheaply. It was her pride and joy, and she went about Covent Garden in her usual way, picking up fruit and vegetables from the gutters. Happiness was hers for a few

days; she would sit in the back of the van and call out to her friends until the smell of the old fruit became too much.

In those days there wasn't a problem parking – but people complained, and the police arrived and told her she must move on or they would confiscate the lot.

'But I can't drive,' she told us. 'I've always had a chauffeur.'

Someone said he would drive her to

'What were you doing at half past seven nearly naked in a churchyard?' 'I was dressing for dinner!'

Kent. He knew an apple orchard in which she could park. When they got there she danced around and said how lovely it was – soon she'd have a kitchen garden and anyone who cared to visit could stay as her guest. 'Don't forget to tell them I'm at my country seat,' she said as she waved goodbye.

Nothing was heard of her for a few weeks, until one day a sad figure wandered into Soho. We gathered around, offering her the cream cakes she loved. 'Oh, I missed the cream pastries – you can't get them in Kent and too much fruit isn't good for one's health! Besides,' she said, 'one should be in town during the Season!'

Weeks later I asked about the van. It seemed the man that drove her there couldn't be found, so one day you may come across an orchard with a van in the middle.

Take me to Leicester square!

One day I was in Bond Street on my way to an important interview. I was dressed and made up and feeling rather pleased with myself.

'Well, my dear,' said a voice. 'Fancy seeing you!'

I turned around and there was Eileen; instead of plastic bags, a lizard handbag, shoes, not the usual plimsolls, and a leather coat with a fur collar. I told her I was in a hurry. 'We could have tea at Fortnum's,' she suggested. 'Nice creamy cakes.' Her eyebrows rose rather wistfully.

'Sorry,' I said. 'Oh well, stop a taxi for me then.' So I did. 'Where to?' asked the driver. Eileen planted one foot inside the open door and went on talking about this and that in a rather loud and cultured voice. The driver got fed up. 'Come on missus, where to?' Eileen hopped into the taxi and announced, 'Take me to Leicester Square, the public conveniences.' She slammed the door and was off, chuckling to herself.

Lies, spies and intrigue

MELANIE MCFADYEAN's *mother Marion, who died in 2007, fled Nazi Germany in 1937 and then worked in the infamous world of black propaganda*

I never really knew what my mother, Marion Whitehorn, née Gutmann, did in the war until TV documentary makers began to seek her out – not only because she was a refugee from Nazi Germany but because she had a particular story which successive film makers always asked her about when they descended on her in her lovely Sussex home: 'Tell us about the drawing you did of Hitler's penis.'

In 1937, at the age of 18, Marion Gutmann fled Germany with her mother, Daisy. Her father, Herbert, the one-time director of the Dresdner Bank (founded by his father), and two older brothers had gone ahead. They took with them a small suitcase each and a few German marks. They had return tickets because they had to keep up the pretence that they had been invited on holiday to the UK, but my mother never saw her childhood home again.

Marion had been classified by the Nazi regime as being neither a 'racial Jew' nor 'Aryan' because although her father was Jewish, her mother was not. She was considered a *Mischling*, first degree; the term given to people who are a 'mixture'. Unlike her two older brothers, one of whom was praised at school for his fine Aryan head shape and profile, my mother had a classic Jewish beauty: high cheek bones, a curved nose and, before it went grey, thick dark hair.

I imagine hearts melted and broke regularly because of that one in a million face. Not that it seems to have made an impression at her tribunal hearings, where as an enemy alien she endured tough questioning before being allowed to do her bit against her persecutors. After three gruelling hearings, she was given permission to work, although she had to report to the police if she wanted to go further than ten miles from London.

Colin McFadyean, her fiancé and my future father, couldn't marry her until her alien status had been resolved. He was away at sea, fighting the Battle of the Atlantic, until the end of 1942, when a

Photograph of Marion Whitehorn by Jane Bown

minor eye injury, sustained on leave while chopping wood, resulted in him being drafted into naval intelligence in London. As a naval officer, he couldn't marry her until her status was resolved. As soon as it was, they got married and, a fluent German speaker, he was detailed to debrief captured U-boat commanders.

Marion, meanwhile, was invited to work for the highly secretive 'black' propaganda programme. Under the

auspices of the Political Warfare Executive (PWE), there were two branches of propaganda – white and black. The most successful and ingenious propaganda was the inspiration of a journalist, Sefton Delmer. Among the intriguing things he thought up and disseminated through the black arm of the propaganda machine were radio frequencies which broadcast under such names as *Soldatensender Calais* and *Atlantiksender*.

Programmes recorded in the UK hit the German airwaves, apparently coming from within Germany itself. Their purpose: to undermine the German public's image of their leaders and create panic and confusion.

Part of the black propaganda programme was a print unit run by Ellic Howe – described by Delmer as 'a printer who had made a special study of German typography and printing techniques. Even before the war he had regularly visited Germany and made a point of collecting specimens of German printing. He carried them all back with him in his baggage – newspapers, tram tickets, commercial and private stationery, business forms, police "wanted" posters, and anything else he could lay his hands on.'

Marion worked in black propaganda from 1943 until the end of 1944. Tommy Harris, the son of an art gallery owner who had given her a job at his gallery, and his wife, Hilda, befriended her, and

Marion liked Kim Philby and found Anthony Blunt 'enchanting'. She didn't, however, have time for 'that shit Guy Burgess'. She said he would get very drunk and they would throw him out into the street. She sensed they were involved in something secret, but even when they were drunk they never talked about what they were up to. She never spoke about her secret propaganda work. But it must have been tempting to tell them the story of her first day in the job.

She was ushered into a darkened room. Several men were sitting round a long table, some in plain clothes, some in uniform. She was not introduced to any of them but was made to swear that she would never divulge anything of the unit's activities; to do so would result in twenty years hard labour. She was handed a post-card which showed a picture of Hitler in lederhosen with his hands cupped in his groin, and was asked to draw a penis as though clutched between his hands. 'Not

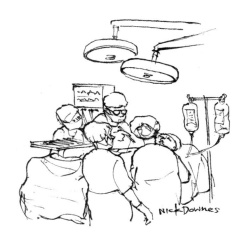

'Look at that poor excuse for a moustache'

In his book, *The Black Game*, Howe describes Elizabeth Friedlander as 'a first-class German graphic artist' and 'a demure spinster in her late thirties'. My mother is not mentioned at all. She said there was a reason for this. On her first day she was invited to lunch by Howe, but when he suggested they sneak off for some postprandial sex, she turned him down flat.

One day, after a lunch break together, Marion went back to Bush House and my father jumped on a bus to return to his office. As he got off, he saw a V-1, or 'doodlebug', making its deadly way through the sky above the Aldwych and, terrified that it would drop where Marion was, hastily jumped back onto another bus.

She was on the stairs, making her way back to her office on the sixth floor, when the bomb landed outside the building. Colin leapt from the bus and ran towards the scene of carnage. Bodies had already been laid out by the time he arrived, frantically looking for Marion's dark curls.

Marion, meanwhile, was picking her way towards the remains of her office. The door was hanging open, the windows had been blown out and glass had pierced the back of a filing cabinet, blasting open its drawers. Top secret material was floating in the air, making its way down through the well of the building and out of the shattered windows onto the street.

Colin was still making his way along the line of dead bodies when Marion appeared before him.

She returned to work two weeks later, but she had had enough of Howe's rudeness and transferred to white propaganda. She later discovered that her uncle, Fritz Gutmann, had been beaten to death in Theresienstadt, while his wife, Louise, died in Auschwitz. My mother was lucky not to have met the same fate.

Marion met a clutch of famous spies at these parties. She liked Kim Philby, and Anthony Blunt was 'enchanting', but she didn't have time for 'that shit Guy Burgess'

it was probably through them that she met Sefton Delmer and Ellic Howe.

Tommy Harris had already been a catalyst in her life in another significant way. One weekend in the spring of 1938, they drove to Paris for a party, where she met another guest – my father. 'Colin and I went to marvellous parties at Tommy and Hilda's,' Marion recalled. What she didn't know until many years later was that Tommy, a painter, also had a secret life as the MI5 agent who controlled 'Garbo', the nickname given to the famous double agent, Juan Pujol. A clutch of famous spies were regular guests at these parties.

'How do you like your tin opened?'

too big, not too small,' she was told.

Though probably the least important bit of work she did, it was the one the TV hacks always went for.

The unit included another refugee, Elizabeth Friedlander, a typographer who knew Germanic typefaces and could recreate them for the forged documentation. They forged a stamp with Himmler's head on it instead of Hitler's, suggesting that Himmler was seeking to overthrow Hitler. They made false identity cards and ration cards to cause confusion. Posters were concocted accusing fictitious SS men of embezzlment or desertion, offering rewards for their capture and designed to waste the Gestapo's time. A forged bank note for use in German armed forces' canteens had a rhyme on the back suggesting it should be used to wipe the Führer's arse; a booklet suggested the flour being given to people was poisonous and could cause impotence. Subversive stickers included one with the double letters of the SS printed into the middle of the word *Scheisse* – shit. The most famous piece of sexual imagery to be unleashed on the German public was of a handsome Afro-Caribbean man and a blue-eyed blonde girl having a good time with their pants down.

The Oldie
65 Newman Street
London WIT 3EG
letters @ theoldie.co.uk

Readers write

Tales of woe, joy and outrage: a dip into the Oldie Towers postbag reveals an entertaining sample of our readership

An unusually minty query

SIR: Can someone explain to me why, despite my using it twice each day, a hard unusable lump continuously appears at the end of my toothpaste tube? It never used to happen. Is this just another way of parting us from our money?
Harry Johnson, via email

Lumley is an actress shock

SIR: I've just read the disgraceful news that you've had the temerity to name Joanna Lumley 'Oldie of the Year 2010' for campaigning for the rights of retired Nepalese Gurkha soldiers wanting to settle in Britain. Well, I've got news for you – she is the least deserving 'oldie' imaginable.

Here's why. In her TV show *Ab Fab* this awful female glamorised drug-taking, smoking, heavy drinking and promiscuity.

That sort of degenerate behaviour is appalling and reckless when presented that way; it is the last thing we need when trying to steer youngsters away from the perils

'Sir: I wish to express my surprise, tinged with joy, that you are still alive'

of all four of those vices, especially drugs. Frankly, her character in that show and the message it sent out to impressionable youngsters was little short of disgraceful.

Shame on you lot.
Bill Johnstone, via email

Not disgusted

SIR: My heart went out to you when reading all the grouchy comments in the letters pages! [*Oldies passim ad nauseam*] Don't worry. I, and I expect many others, like *The Oldie* just as it is. Perhaps we should say so more frequently.

If, occasionally, there is an article that bores me I turn the page and hope the culprit will do better next time.

And so, Mr Ingrams, THANK YOU for all your dedication, and carry on just as before.
Trienie Henfrey, Feltham

Even less disgusted

SIR: This is my reply to the miserable so-and-sos who have written all those moaning letters to *The Oldie*.

Oh, *what* is the matter with people today?

Those grumpy old bastards who write in to say that Kit Wright is 'ridiculous' (no, he is NOT), 'this cartoon's in bad

---

In 2010 a cartoon by Larry, reproduced in The Oldie Book of Cartoons, precipitated a flurry of letters from readers...

An acceptable face of humour?

SIR: We were given a copy of *The Oldie Book of Cartoons* for Christmas.

When we noticed the cartoon on the back cover we were appalled. We tried hard to find the relevance, let alone the humour. We looked up 'Larry' and it appears that he is now deceased, so we are unable to consult him as to the meaning or merit of this cartoon. We have shown it to several thinking people of all ages and nobody has been able to account for the cartoon or feel that it has any place in any kind of publication. We are embarrassed to have this book in our house. I would not want anyone to see it lying around and think that we think it is OK.

Would you please explain what you found humorous about this particular cartoon, which seems to have been selected for special treatment, as not only is it inside in black and white on page 146, but also in colour on the back cover.

The friend who sent us this book was unaware of this cartoon, and she is extremely embarrassed.
Margaret and Michael Judd, Massachusetts

Lost in translation?

SIR: I noted with interest the comments made by Margaret and Michael Judd in the last edition of *The Oldie* regarding

The cartoon which appalled

the controversial Larry cartoon.

As Americans, the Judds have probably never heard of Thomas the Tank Engine, and thus did not realise that the cartoon was intended as a darkly ironic comment on the crass commercialisation that has befallen the Rev W Awdrey's famous creation.
Owen Morgan, Worcestershire

That controversial cartoon again...

SIR: Further to the letter from Margaret and Michael Judd and the cartoon reproduced in the March *Oldie*, the only relevance I can detect is a satire, possibly distasteful depending on one's point of view, on Hitler's use of the railways to send Jews to their deaths in cattle wagons. The father and son, if that is indeed what they are, are clearly not entering a passenger carriage!
Joe Hayward, Stanmore, Middlesex

taste', and other such rot. And as for 'BAD language' – for Pete's sake, GROW UP!

Please note that not all of us feel the same way.
Jayne Osborn, via email

Urn respect

SIR: The 'Bodies' article from *Oldie* 261 (September 2010) reminded me of the countless corpses I dealt with during thirty years in the Metropolitan Police Service. On one occasion, however, it was the ashes that I had to deal with, when an official from Hackney Council gave me a sealed brass urn which he had found on the local rubbish tip. Over many days I contacted various crematoria and asked them to check their records against the reference number stamped into the base of the urn. I eventually got the answer I hoped for – the name and address of the deceased. Even better, when I checked the voters' register, I found the widow was still shown at the address.

So one morning, in my Sergeant's uniform, with a rather heavy heart, I visited the address with hubby's ashes discreetly hidden in my large briefcase. A nice oldie answered the door and I explained that I had some rather sad news to give her. I suggested that a chat over a cup of tea would be a good idea. She made a strong cuppa and then with the utmost reverence I placed the urn on the coffee table. 'Is that all you've come about?' she said. 'He's been sitting on the mantelpiece for years and I got so fed up of looking at him that I decided to chuck him out!'
Alan Boyd, Kent

Oldies in the waiting room

SIR: A couple of years ago I took some *Oldies* to my doctor's surgery and put

'To whom it may concern...'

them on the table. Collecting the prescription two days later I saw that they had gone. I asked one of the assistants and she said, 'Oh, you put them there? Well I don't think that's funny. We get a lot of old people in here and they wouldn't think that was very nice.'
Barry Barker, via email

SIR: I used to leave old magazines in our local hospital, but ''ealth and safety' have decreed that they are a danger and must be removed.
S M Hoare, via email

Ed in still with us shocker

SIR: I wish to express my surprise, tinged with joy, that you are still alive. Forgive me, but I assumed you were at the worst dead and at the best 'out of commission'. I have recently enjoyed the repeats of *Beachcomber* on BBC7 and just now was watching a re-run of a Gerald Scarfe documentary from a few years back and there you were, so I Googled you to find out what became of you and it appears that nothing became of you. Nothing fatal anyway.
M Bicker, via email

Stop that racket!

SIR: The pianist Arthur Rubinstein always stayed at the Savoy when in

London, having a suite with a concert grand installed. One time the manager came to see him: 'Mr Rubinstein, the guests in the room next to yours are complaining about the sound of the piano, what can I do?'
'Charge them double.'
John Amis, London

'Joanna Lumley is the least deserving Oldie of the Year. In her TV show Ab Fab, this awful female glamorised drug-taking, smoking, heavy drinking and promiscuity'

The kindness of lawyers

SIR: A few weeks ago I saw an elderly gentleman parking an old BMW saloon, registration mark LIBEL. I was so impressed that I said to him, 'That number plate would be worth a fortune to Carter-Ruck, the leading libel lawyers.' He smiled and said: 'My son is a solicitor and Carter-Ruck liked him so much that he gave it to him.' The number plate came off one of Peter Carter-Ruck's cherished possessions, a Rolls-Royce Silver Shadow.

Despite being the scourge of *Private Eye* and many newspapers, frequently in relation to money, there was a kind and generous side to his character, obviously.
Alan Boyd, Bromley

A punter writes...

SIR: Would you please refrain from calling your subscribers 'punters'.
Jim Redshaw, Shrewsbury

Audience

Sixty portraits by Evelyn Williams

I n the ghost tunnel at the fairground, an image will leap out of the darkness and scream at you, to disappear into the blackness again. So a portrait should jolt in the same way – should have an immediate sense of presence that startles and impinges, skinned of pretence.

In *Audience* these people sit in a theatre, each isolated from the other. Each seeing a different play according to their own response. As they look at the stage we do not know what they are thinking but we, the spectators, are left with the uneasy feeling they are seeing and judging us.

When painting these sixty portraits of imaginary people I was sometimes surprised to pass people in the street whom I recognised from the painting. If a portrait doesn't have a life of its own, it has failed.

EVELYN WILLIAMS

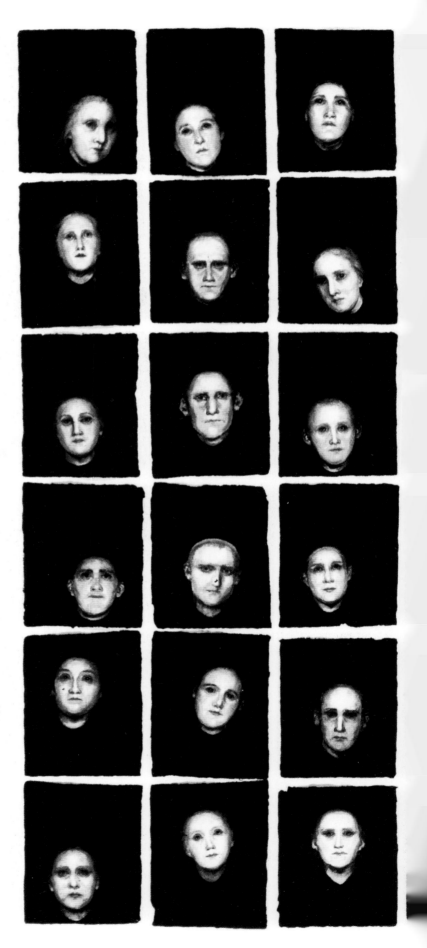

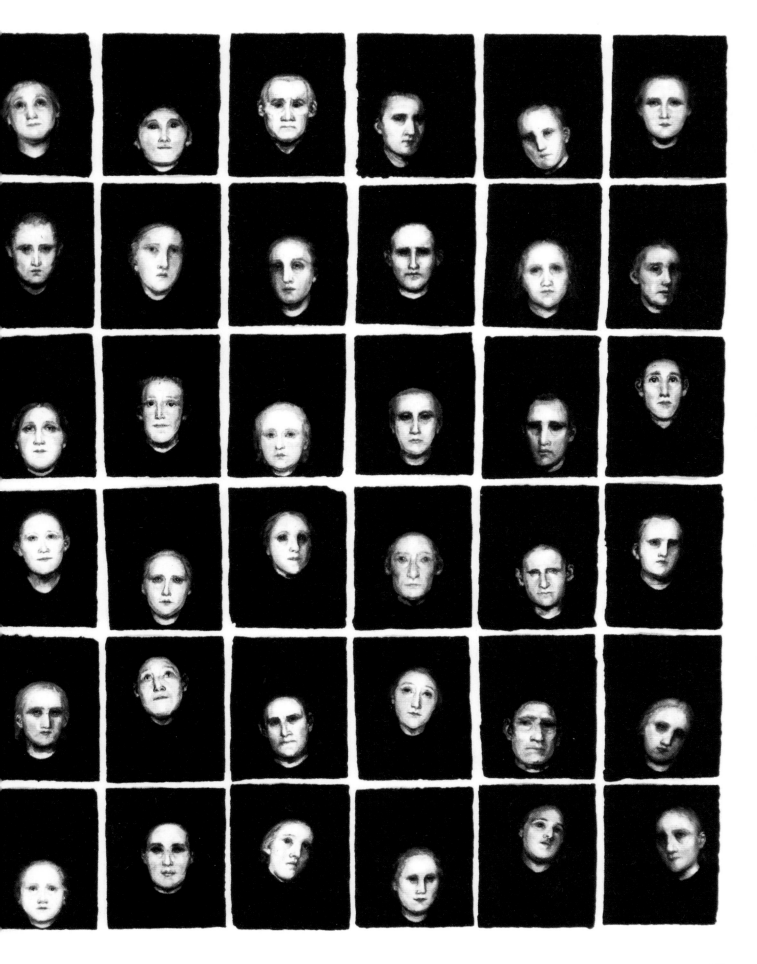

La chambre anglaise

BARRY POSNER *offers an invaluable guide for Brits staying in France. With illustrations by* **ARTHUR ROBINS**

In every moderately sized hotel in France there is one room that *le directeur* knows very well should have been bricked up the day the builders finished and downed tools. A bonus is paid to the staff if they manage to persuade a luckless guest to stay long enough to warrant a bill the next morning. This guest is invariably English.

The French are of the opinion that the English are the least complaining of all their visitors. They are right. We are not complainers. It is for this reason that my thesis, *la chambre anglaise,* is just that; there is no need to translate it into any other language.

When you arrive at your hotel, in your GB-labelled *voiture,* the first warning sign

is that there is nobody visible at reception, but instead sounds of Gallic gaiety emanate from the kitchens. Venturing nervously in that direction, you invariably spy the sous-chef in a modest clinch with *la réceptionniste,* even if it is only 3 pm.

At this point you render the Brit's first acquired and most significant words in French, 'pardonnez-moi'. You are already apologising.

The *réceptionniste* prised from the arms of her amour, and the registration process concluded, one ventures, 'Can someone help with the baggage?' 'Only me M'sieur,' says the pretty but frail young lady, not much taller than your suitcases. Gallantly you carry your own up a minimum of six short staircases, separated by long corridors – a global SatNav system will be needed to get back to reception. In your sweaty palpitating discomfort you drop the bags on the floor and take stock. The room has charm... superficially.

The View. Although the hotel is in a commanding position with rooms facing over the valley below, your room is at the back of the hotel, the only window being six feet away from a blank stone wall across a wretched alleyway. This is one of the cardinal signs of *la chambre anglaise* and requires immediate action if the *Entente* is going to remain *Cordiale.*

The next favourite position for *la chambre* is immediately over the kitchens, where you can enjoy the sounds and mouth-watering smells of the kitchen from your bed at all hours.

The Wardrobe was already rubbish when it was made in 1850 and is so terrifyingly dark inside that one

expects the skeleton of a long-forgotten *mousquetaire* to emerge when opened. The catch will either work open or shut, but never both.

Light fittings have special bulbs of a maximum of 15 watts. Combat this by carrying powerful wattage bulbs bought on a previous trip to substitute during your stay. This simple ploy gives you immense satisfaction every time you switch the light on, and also reduces the depression caused by the view of the blank wall or the brooding wardrobe.

The Bathroom. Most French bathrooms have a flexible tube with a showerhead attached, which lies on the bottom

The French are of the opinion that the English are the least complaining race

of the bath to no obvious purpose.

It never occurred to anybody that if this fitting was secured two metres above the bath, it could clean you quickly and efficiently. But this would require a shower curtain. There is no such thing in France and no French word for it. The bathroom will also have a combination of a blocked or desperately slow drain, a toilet tank that takes a day to refill, and an exciting plastic soap dispenser that never dispenses anything.

So what to do now? There is only one option which does not come naturally. Complain. Do not be discouraged by the thought of dragging your bags back to reception. Do it and help our Island Nation to ultimately integrate more successfully into Europe.

BRAVE NEW WORLD

Change of address

Complaining is the French national occupation and may generate grudging admiration in between the expressive Gallic shrugs. Once, when faced with a spiral staircase to climb three floors to our room – with our luggage, naturally – we were able to reduce the climb to two on appeal. On another occasion we were moved and housed next to the lift-shaft. The lift had an antique sofa and a spectacular *fin-de-siècle* mirror, but unfortunately rattled as much from side to side as it moved vertically. As a vintage car owner I felt a familiar understanding and warm affection for it as it struggled by. Are we not a tolerant race indeed?

The experience of *la chambre anglaise* has never discouraged my wife and me from returning to France year after year. After all, a few extra light bulbs take up very little room in your luggage, and I'm getting progressively better at sitting down in the bath to take a shower.

Vive la différence!
Vive la tolérance!

THE ONE THING everyone knows about cyberspace is that, like ordinary space, it goes on forever. But could that one thing be wrong? It seemed so, as far as the internet is concerned, when in February 2011 it was revealed that the internet was, to all intents, full up.

The world wide web ran out of space when the last free IP (Internet Protocol) address was allocated by the Number Resource Organisation, the body which creates internet addresses. An IP address is the unique series of numbers assigned to each computer or website, and already 4.3 billion have been used. But due to the huge number of smart phones, iPads and laptops going online, that provision was exhausted.

In one way this isn't a problem, because a new system, IPv6, has been created, which will provide 34 trillion addresses and should last until Armageddon. The problem is that websites using the new system may not be accessible to computers with older software.

Technically, the internet is just a large number of computers connected to each other, so it would only run out of space if all the individual memories of all the computers were full. That's unlikely to happen, and instead it's growing all the time. Indeed, few of us really appreciate just how enormous it is. One intriguing revelation has been the existence of the 'dark web' – a deep, hidden online environment which contains terrorist guides, pornography, pirated books, political samizdat and secretive networks which people can use without leaving tracks. These websites are inaccessible to search engines like Google and a huge number can only be accessed by people who know the correct codes. The dark web is estimated to be as much as five hundred times the size of the 'surface web' seen by you and me – which makes you wonder just how many people out there must be using it.

JANE THYNNE

'You don't have to wear the burka if you don't want to – it was only a suggestion'

A pop to the local

BEN MALLALIEU's *mother once made an unexpected entrance into her friendly local pub...*

One afternoon in the summer of 1962, my mother drove into the pub. The car was a ten-year-old Daimler and the pub was The Old Fisherman in Shabbington on the border of Buckinghamshire and Oxfordshire. A narrow road led straight down from the top of the hill, with a steep bank rising on the right-hand side and a drop into the River Thame on the other. At the bottom, the road turned left over a narrow bridge, with a barn immediately ahead and The Fisherman to the right. Halfway down the hill, she put her foot on the brake pedal but found it was flat on the floor; then a cyclist began to cross the bridge from the other direction. My mother's first thought was to drive into the barn, but fearing she might demolish it entirely she turned right and hit the corner of the pub, coming to a halt just in front of the bar. Fortunately, being mid-afternoon, it was empty. Both my mother and the elkhound who had been sitting on the passenger seat were unhurt, but the dog never really enjoyed car journeys after that.

Driving down the hill 45 years later, the road and the bridge have hardly changed, and the narrow river is still lined with pollarded willows that appear not to have grown at all. But the village, the pub and the car we are driving in are very different.

The Daimler was heavy, slow and, even in its time, old-fashioned: one of the last cars to have running-boards. But it was very comfortable, smelling of burnt oil and old leather, and the doors

She hit the corner of the pub, coming to a halt just in front of the bar...

shut with a satisfying clunk. Due to its fluid flywheel, it would creep without any judder from stationary to a funereal walking pace and then proceed without undue haste to a maximum of about 75 mph at which it could glide effortlessly all day, or until the radiator boiled. Acceleration and braking were not its strong points (nor, at under 15 miles to

the gallon, was fuel consumption) but on that afternoon it would have looked rather grand, having just been resprayed very dark green with a fine gold line hand-painted along the bonnet. It was easy back then to have cars repaired: what was then known as Morris's was often on strike and its craftsmen were happy to earn extra money, taking more pride in their work than they ever did at Cowley.

In those days, The Fisherman was still a rough country pub. Many of the regulars had moved to the area after leaving the services to find work at the car factory. Other pub regulars still worked on the land, including an old shepherd with a white beard and a smock, surely one of the last of his kind in the Home Counties. Old and new residents drank happily side by side and played together in the pub's cricket team. My parents liked it for the friendliness of all the locals, and most Saturday lunchtimes in the school holidays my sister and I would sit outside in the car and occasionally be brought bottles of lukewarm Vimto and packets of crisps with twists of salt in blue wrappers. The landlord was a man called Dick, who in those days was considered a 'character', though now he would be regarded as a dangerous alcoholic whom no brewery would leave in charge of a pub.

Forty-five years later, The Old Fisherman is still a pub but most of its revenue comes from food (it was crisps or nothing in the Daimler days). The place has been smartened up, and the barn has been converted into an extra dining-room. The menu belongs to a particular time and market niche. A dish like 'New Zealand green-lipped mussels *au gratin*' would not have been found on a menu ten years ago, nor is it likely to be in ten years time. The Fisherman serves better than average pub food but does not quite aspire to 'gastropub' status: 'char-grilled' occurs five times on the menu but 'locally sourced' not at all. The lamb comes with 'merlot and mint sauce' and not 'merlot and mint *jus*'. They serve a range of coffees, including the uninviting-sounding 'floater coffee'. Portions are large and business brisk, the landlord sober and hard-working. I told him my mother had once driven into the pub. 'Oh yes,' he said with a certain finality. I never discovered whether the incident had become part of local folk lore or had been forgotten entirely.

Brief encounters

NIGEL FOUNTAIN *looks at the lives of others*

Alicia wears big round glasses and her hair, scrupulously pulled back and ordered, cascades out from beyond a clip. Alicia is engaging, pretty, quirky, golden brown, nervous, smiles a lot, and, as anchor-person of her show, juggles stories, provides footnotes, repetitions and on-set rewrites.

Near Olympic City in East London, we, and her three suitcases, are sharing a bench. She is wearing metallic eyeshadow which shows signs of flaking. She is, she says, sort of self-employed. I ask her how old she is. 'How old do you think?' and I say about 23. 'About 23,' she says. 'That sounds good.' I tick off 28, but I could be wrong.

I ask about the suitcases. 'I am staying at *an* accommodation,' she says. 'And I don't feel very safe leaving my things there. I have been advised, by the Metropolitan Police, to keep them with me until I can change the locks, and find some sort of alarm system – rather than leaving my things there and being ignorant of a situation that is not safe. If I have suspicions of somebody, better to be safe than sorry, and going home and finding my cosmetics have been tampered with.'

Alicia says her birthplace was Romford, but then relocates it to Italy. She just had to go to hospital here, she explains, because that was where her mother was from. Her parents are quite famous, they know celebrities, she says, and she had been brought up within the world of music, entertainment and dance.

'I actually have to have a formal invitation to visit them,' she says. 'They live in West London very close to Buckingham Palace. It's not that they don't want to see me, it's just – I was actively taken away

from them when I was a child. I've got three brothers and a sister. They're older than me. I don't see them as often as I'd like to. They managed to get on with life without me for so long. Growing up without them, for twenty-something years, has been hard – the amount of agony and pain. I was looked after by a family, a husband and wife, foster parents as it were – they did a very good job of it.'

Her parents are quite famous, Alicia says. 'I have to have a formal invitation to visit them...'

Alicia got pregnant with her first child while she was at school in Essex, moved into rented accommodation and worked from home. She says she has a 'good average' of five children – and looks after her friends' children too, godchildren. 'They like me. Especially when it gets to birthdays and Christmas,' she says, and laughs.

She studied law at college, she says, and there have been many other jobs, in travel, promoting shows, with a drinks company, a film outfit and there was a factory in Bow. 'That was interesting, but they couldn't keep me because the production line was working too fast. They would have loved me to stay.' On her last project she was working on a few soundtracks, she says.

One of her daughters shares a birthday with Beyoncé, which Alicia thinks is significant. 'She is just a child, but she is pretty well into the industry whether she likes it or not. But I don't want her growing up on the idea that, because

she's got a lot more skills than a lot of other children, she has to be that much more of a show-off.' She looks at me and I nod affirmation. 'She has to keep it more natural and God-given. I don't want her to be caught up in the limelight.'

After a while she says that, to tell the truth, she only found out three or four years ago who her real parents were. 'I've been told to put a letter together and send it to them and see where it goes from there. That is advice from friends, who have known the solution, being involved in the law industry. It is quite complicated, because there is a chance of me being rejected by them.'

I ask her if she is lonely and she says that is always questionable, always questionable, and she is always missing them. 'Is there anybody you trust?' I say.

'At the moment, other than God and some of my male friends, sort of like husbands, no.'

We wrap up. 'Thank you,' she says, and smiles.

'Is there a reason my peas are touching the mashed potatoes?'

Reithian double standards

As architect of the BBC, Lord Reith's standards were of the highest integrity – but at home he was a bully and a tyrant. His daughter MARISTA LEISHMAN talked to JENNIE ERDAL about how she survived family life

As a boy, John Reith often walked in Kelvingrove Park in Glasgow, sniffing the air for divine messages borne on the breeze. The northerly wind, which blew down from Ben Lomond, was deemed especially propitious. By far the clearest message transmitted to young Reith was that he was destined for great things. When, in 1922, he became general manager of the new British Broadcasting Company, he believed 'the Almighty was there in my receiving that job and was there in the execution of it'.

Whether the Almighty was also there in the family home is doubtful. 'John Reith found it hard to love his children for their own sake,' writes his daughter Marista Leishman in the prologue to *My Father: Reith of the BBC*. She paints a vivid portrait of an autocrat and a bully, a narcissist in public life and a tyrant at home, a tortured man, riven by contradictions, disappointed in himself and even more so in others. His rages were legendary: he shouted at the servants, flogged the dog and humiliated his wife.

Reith's daughter is the living proof that you can survive damage inflicted in your early years and go on to live a good and useful life. You expect her to be scarred and dysfunctional, but she's open and full of life. A few days after her 75th birthday in 2007, sitting in the conservatory of her bonny Highland cottage near Pitlochry, we talked about her memoir and how it came to be written. Marista Leishman tells me she has always been a scribbler, filling notebooks throughout her life, but this memoir of her father was of a different order. 'I knew by instinct that I needed to wait a full term, as it were, till the old resentments had burned away a bit and as much objectivity as possible had crept in. You don't come out from under straightaway.' Was there perhaps an element of wanting to put the record straight? Leishman's honesty is refreshing: 'Our motives are never really pure – I would be foolish to deny it.'

Her memoir is full of bite, yet told without bitterness, and you sense she is striving to get it the way it really was. 'One becomes more forgiving in later years, more accepting, because by this stage one is no longer struggling to find one's own identity.'

Since her father left nothing to chance, Marista's identity – together with that of her older brother – was also ordained: the boy was to become Prime Minister, she Head Wren (and concert pianist on the side). Educated by governesses at home till she was fourteen, Marista was then sent to boarding school – St George's, Ascot. This marked the beginning of her 'getting out from under'. (Meanwhile, her older brother sensibly became a forester in Perthshire.) At St Andrews University she studied English and Philosophy, met her future husband Murray Leishman, and 'stepped free'.

Not without a bit of a fight, however, since marriage was regarded by her father as a monstrous betrayal. Of what did this treachery consist? Surely permanent spinsterhood was not part of Reith's great plan for her? His reasoning was much more bizarre: although his family had failed to live up to his own high standards, the unit was nevertheless indissoluble. 'It was that ghastly business of *we shall all be together in heaven*,' says Leishman. 'Reith's family, quite simply, could not be married into.'

Secure in one another, the couple went ahead and married, and Murray Leishman promptly joined Reith's infamous Hate List, jostling for position with Churchill, Mountbatten, Montgomery and Eden. The Hate List, though a serious exercise in loathing, was also a means of shocking people, of attracting attention to himself – 'He demeaned himself further by not even realising it.'

Mr Leishman, as Reith always called him, started his professional life as a minister in the Church of Scotland before becoming a psychotherapist – which 'made us better able to deflect the brickbats that regularly came our way.' Humour and compassion also helped. 'My husband and I have done a lot of work together on my father, asking ourselves: how could this be? We have hypothesised all over the place, and that in itself is extremely liberating.'

Psychologists tell us that bad things are passed down the line. Had she worried about 'becoming her father' and perhaps revisiting ills done to her on her own children? 'I always had one clear objective: that they should be free, autonomous individuals. And the surprise was to discover the joy in children, the shared delights. My father was terrified of children – it was seen and not heard with him.'

Reith's visits to his children's nursery were attended by great formality – 'like a state visit' – and consisted for the most part in the awkward singing of hymns at bedtime. 'Awkward' is a word Leishman uses regularly to describe how it was, growing up with Reith. It is a kind word in the circumstances.

Her mother Muriel is a rather shadowy figure in the book, yet in a sense she is the real hero, not least because, unlike Marista and her brother, she was unable to get away. She was rather timid, reduced to a nervous wreck by her husband. Leishman recounts one of her father's many cutting remarks: 'I can't give Muriel a book for her birthday because she's got one.' In a different man, this might have been construed as

Opposite: Lord Reith with his wife and children
Above: Marista Leishman today

humour. But Reith didn't do humour.

He did do hypocrisy, however. As you would expect of a man raised in the austerity of a Free Church of Scotland manse, Reith disapproved of adultery and liked to practise 'the language of vituperation' while cultivating an image of integrity and incorruptibility. But privately – and not so privately sometimes – he had a series of extra-marital relationships, following in the great Scottish tradition of the Justified Sinner, so vividly drawn by James Hogg nearly two hundred years before. In dealing with this side of her

She paints a vivid portrait of Lord Reith as an autocrat and a bully, a tortured man, riven by contradictions

father, Leishman deploys many of the same skills as Hogg: profound insight, black humour and deep compassion.

At the age of twenty-three, Reith had also become infatuated with Charlie Bowser, a beautiful sixteen-year-old boy. 'I would be slow to call it homosexuality,' says Leishman. 'Here were two lost young men – particularly the older one – starved of sympathy, affection and attention. It was an all-embracing form of deprivation, as severe as malnutrition. I think it had to do with appalling loneliness.'

Leishman writes very persuasively and amusingly about her father's assumed 'one-to-one relationship with the Almighty', whose aspirations for the BBC – 'to educate, to inform and to entertain'

– coincided exactly with Reith's own. 'The Almighty was his own construct – and the relationship was an excluding one. These aspirations were far-reaching, so he could easily line up the Almighty to assist in the whole process and ennoble it.' Had she managed to keep the faith herself, I wondered? And had she ever discussed religion with her father? 'No, we didn't talk about anything really.' For Reith, Leishman thinks, the heavenly father was totally confused with his earthly father. 'I myself never made that mistake because all the signs were rather in the opposite direction. What grabbed me about religion was the music, and it took a long time to realise they were separate things. Murray was a minister when we married, and that removed any final blinkers. Congregational life was not for either of us.'

Reith was a consummate actor and loved showing off. There is a comic vignette in the memoir when he is called upon to deputise for the Queen at the Palace of Holyrood, where he adored being bowed and curtsied to. Afterwards he wrote in his diary: 'For once I found myself adequately circumstanced.' (He later approached Lord Longford to try and get a higher grading in the peerage – Viscount would have suited him nicely.) With this degree of hubris, it was surely odd that he spoke constantly about failure, never about success. 'But when you cast yourself as a failure, people take notice of that.' Nothing to do with humility then? 'No. As Malcolm Muggeridge said, he was splendidly cast as himself.' Muggeridge also said he found him, 'in a weird way, loveable' and talked of his greatness being attended by 'so many intimations of littleness'.

After all that has been revealed, is it still meaningful to talk of 'the Reithian standard'? 'It hasn't lost any of its impact. John Reith's powers, at their best, were for releasing new capabilities in people and enlarging the spectrum of human accomplishment.'

Reith resigned in tears from the BBC in 1938, and was filled with regret for the rest of his life. 'There was pathos there. The lost child was never far away. I pitied him.' This deeply flawed man was fond of saying: 'I never learned to live.' The same cannot be said of his daughter.

• *My Father: Reith of the BBC* is published by St Andrew Press, £8.99 PB

In memoriam gifts
For Cancer, Prevention is Key

DO!

✓ Be physically active

✓ Practise safe sex

✓ Eat five to nine servings of fruit and vegetables daily

✓ Drink green tea

✓ Maintain a healthy body weight

✓ Avoid job-related chemical exposures

DON'T!

✗ Smoke

✗ Expose yourself excessively to the sun

✗ Consume excessive amounts of red meat

✗ Drink excessive amounts of alcohol

✗ Use talcum powder

✗ Consume excessive amounts of animal fats

A recent study found that non-smokers who followed advice for cancer prevention had a lower risk of death from cancer, heart disease and all causes. *Cancer Epidemiology Biomarkers & Prevention, April 2011*

Our sacred mission: the prevention of cancer

For donations, *in memoriam* gifts, legacies

Cancer Prevention Research Trust

231 Roehampton Lane, London SW15 4LB
Tel: 020 8785 7786   Fax: 020 8785 6466
E-mail: mail@cancerpreventionresearch.org.uk

Registered Charity No. 265985

www.cancerpreventionresearch.org.uk

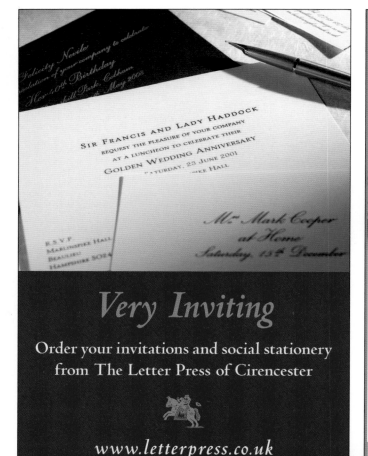

The Oldie EMPORIUM

BEDDING

Arelle Natural Fibre Fleece Blankets
For Winter Warmth in Total Comfort

Fine Merino wool, cashmere, camel and more

Cosy texture that provides warmth and support

Stabilises temperature and humidity

Relieves aches and pains

Sleep Well and wake up really refreshed

Contact us now for your free sample

www.arelleblankets.com

freephone 0800 389 3597

STAIRLIFTS

Stairlifts
Free Phone 0800 046 3438

Nationwide suppliers of quality stairlift solutions for all budgets
- New stairlifts from **£1300**
- Reconditioned stairlifts from **£800**
- Fully comprehensive range of curved stairlifts
- We also repair, service and warranty all other stailifts

www.stairlifts.uk.net

CLOTHING

Doing what comes naturally...
Many natural and traditional items that are fast becoming difficult to find, including:
English made sheepskin slippers, hats, and mittens.
100% cotton nightshirts and nightdresses.
Linen towels, tea-towels, and bedding.
Pure wool underwear, socks & bed-socks.
Superior shaving brushes, safety razors, etc.
The purest soaps and suchlike from France and Norfolk, and as they always say much, much more!

ASK FOR OUR FREE CATALOGUE
OR BROWSE AND ORDER ON OUR WEBSITE

ELM HOUSE PRODUCTS
St. Margaret - Harleston - Norfolk - IP20 0PJ
Tel: 01986 783833 - email: sales@elmhouseproducts.co.uk
www.elmhouseproducts.co.uk

TRAVEL

CRETE: SEASIDE HIDEAWAYS AMONG THE OLIVES
Hush! Shimmering landscape, distant hills, nearby sea. Traditional Cottage, House & Villa, with all mod-cons: air-conditioning, free wi-fi, TV/DVD, microwaves, proper plumbing, barbecues & pool. Quiet tavernas just 300m away, beaches 650m, pretty fishing harbour and shops 1.5 km. Wonderful wildflowers in spring, serious sun in summer, a long warm autumn.
DR D H R NAYLOR:
0115 960 5629 ☎ 0781 683 1565
www.seaside-hideaways.com

CLOTHING

Denny Andrews
Comfortable clothes
Made in India from pure cotton, silk or wool in styles that don't date; kaftans, waistcoats, dresses, full skirts, nightwear and lots more..... ask for a catalogue
Denny Andrews, Clock House, Coleshill, Swindon SN6 7PT
www.dennyandrews.co.uk
or 01793 762476

BOOKS AND PUBLISHING

Ripping Yarns Bookshop
355 Archway Road, London, N6 4EJ
(opposite Highgate tube station)

vintage bookshop with wide range of general stock: fiction and non-fiction

Tues-Fri 12-5, Sat 10-5, Sun 11-4
www.rippingyarns.co.uk
0208 341 6111   yarns@rippingyarns.co.uk

JEWELLERY

THE ELEGANCE AND ALLURE OF CLASSIC JEWELLERY BY JON'S JEWELS

WWW.JONSJEWELS.CO.UK

CDS/DVDS

ANY CAMCORDER TAPE VHS OR BETAMAX TAPE COPIED TO DVD FOR £10
CINE FILMS -ANY AGE/GAUGE/SIZE TO DVD & blu-ray
FREE TRIAL OFFER
TEL. 01454 772857 (24 hours)
WWW.memoriesonvideo.co.uk

HOUSE

DAYSGONEBY
Traditional Wooden Clothes Horse
from £48 delivered
01983 822806
www.daysgoneby.co.uk

WANTED

Record Collections Wanted
ROCK, JAZZ, PSYCH, BEATLES, OBSCURE, FOLK, SIXTIES - LP'S - 7" AND EP'S
Best cash prices - anywhere in the uk
Call Chris McGranaghan - 07795 548242
Email cmcgrn@btinternet.com

SOCIETIES

The Book of Common Prayer is Your Heritage
Help us retain its continued use for this and future generations.
Join the Prayer Book Society.
To find out more about the work of a society that advances a centuries-old spiritual gem.

Join on line at www.pbs.org.uk or ring
Ian Woodhead – 01380 870384

The Prayer Book Society Registered Charity No. 1099295. Co. Limited by Guarantee No.4786973

'Have you ever thought of becoming a traffic warden?'